worry-free living

RYUHO OKAWA

First published in Japanese as *Kokoro Wo Iyasu Stree-free No Kofujuron*
by IRH Press Co. Ltd, in 2012

Published by Westland Books, a division of Nasadiya Technologies Private Limited, in 2025

No. 269/2B, First Floor, 'Irai Arul', Vimalraj Street, Nethaji Nagar, Alapakkam Main Road, Maduravoyal, Chennai 600095

Westland and the Westland logo are the trademarks of Nasadiya Technologies Private Limited, or its affiliates.

ISBN: 9789360457297

10 9 8 7 6 5 4 3 2

The views and opinions expressed in this work are the author's own and the facts are as reported by him, and the publisher is in no way liable for the same.

Book design by Karla Baker
Cover image by lenkis_art/Shutterstock.com

Printed at Thomson Press India Private Limited

worry-free living

LET GO OF STRESS
AND LIVE IN
PEACE AND HAPPINESS

RYUHO OKAWA

contents

CHAPTER TWO

Improving Your Relationships

CHAPTER THREE

A Heart of Blessing

preface

The worries people face must be as numerous as the people in this world. It is the job of the religious leader to extract the most common elements from within these worries and offer ways to deal with them.

This book was compiled mainly from lectures I have given to members of our local temples in the regional cities in Japan, where I spoke candidly from a relaxed standpoint about my basic ideas.

I will be delighted if this book becomes a guide to help you, time and again, in your efforts to understand your mind and discover the meaning of our life in this world.

Ryuho Okawa
Founder and CEO
Happy Science Group

CHAPTER ONE

coping with stress

1

How to Deal with Relationship Stress

Stress Is the Main Cause of Many Modern Problems

The topic of managing stress transcends religion, and the ability to manage stress is a blessing to everyone living today. This topic is probably of great significance to not only Japanese, but also Americans and people from other countries.

The problems we face in today's world vary, but no matter how we describe them, the distress they cause us is the result of stress. Some of you who are reading this may just want to find out how to deal with stress; you may feel that's all you need to know to achieve enlightenment in the modern world. And you may believe that you don't need to belong to any organization such as Happy Science to achieve enlightenment. But things don't work that way.

This chapter will certainly give you a glimpse of the world of enlightenment, but please know that just reading it won't help you achieve a higher state of awareness immediately. Behind what I discuss in this chapter, there is a deeply religious, profound, and mystic background.

This chapter is based on a talk I gave at the Happy Science Matsudo temple located in a suburban city in Chiba Prefecture in Japan. Before the lecture, I asked the audience to respond to questionnaires about the kinds of worries they had and what they felt stressed about.

The results revealed that their two main concerns were personal relationships and financial or monetary problems, followed by some concerns about old age. We would probably get similar results if we asked people on the street. These are relatively basic but essential issues that many people want to know about, so I would like to offer solutions to these kinds of problems in this chapter.

Among the people who filled in the questionnaire, the most common issue they felt stressed out about was relationship issues, specifically with the people they worked with in their jobs or within an organization.

In general, employers measure and classify employees using a range of criteria, such as expertise, educational and work backgrounds, past achievements, and the number of years the employee has worked for the company. Employers use these criteria to assign each employee to appropriate positions. And this is where employees face relationship issues.

My Experience of Conflicts with a Senior Colleague

I remember feeling considerably stressed out during the six years I worked for a trading company during my twenties. When I think back on that experience now, however, I feel completely free from the stress I had back then. All the issues and worries that I felt stressed out about have disappeared. There is not a single unsolved problem that I have carried over to this day, which means that I have not stayed the same myself. I have been taking on new challenges one after another, so what was once a cause of stress or worry for me has all passed like a flow of river and has become trivial.

Back then, several alumni of the University of Tokyo, my alma mater, were working for the same trading company. One of them, who was my senior colleague, was the main source of my distress. Now that I look back, however, I feel very grateful to this colleague for putting me through the mill, because that experience made me who I am today. He probably felt that he should give me a tough-love lesson by pointing out my weaknesses piercingly, as if to deliberately stick pins into my heart. Thanks to his tough-love lessons, though, I was able to gain wisdom and truly learn a lot.

At the same time, there was very good chance that my colleague treated me harshly simply to relieve his own stress. It would most likely have become a big issue had he treated others in the same way. He probably expected me to bear and listen to his unreasonable demands because I was younger and we had graduated from the same department at the same university. In any case, he offered many tough lessons to train me.

For example, I remember that when I helped with the hiring of new graduates, he severely derided me for recruiting a fair number of talented new graduates from my alma mater. He said something like, "You'll suffer later if you hire so many capable people now. Don't you know that those who join the company five to ten years after you will all eventually become your tough rivals?" I was shocked to hear him say that, because such a thought had never crossed my mind. I simply thought that my job was to hire talented people who could contribute to the development of the company, so I dedicated myself to recruiting capable and intelligent people.

I was especially skilled at hiring candidates who had received offers from other companies. As was proved later on, when I started my own organization, Happy Science, I could win over even those who had received offers from many other leading companies. Hiring was one of the assignments given to me back then, in addition to my regular work. Although I didn't receive much compensation for this type of work, I was happy to help, simply because I enjoyed it. So when that senior colleague shared his thought with me, I remember thinking, "I see. I guess wise people see things differently. I didn't think that far ahead."

Another case of his tough-love lesson had to do with my spiritual powers, which I already possessed at the time. But I didn't openly share that fact with my coworkers. I did tell a few people I could trust about the spiritual phenomena I experienced. But somehow the rumor spread, and my senior colleague heard about it. I remember him scolding me fiercely, saying things like, "You need to repent! Take back all the spiritual things you said!" He tried to force me to deny the spiritual phenomena I had experienced.

Now, I often talk about the "sunny" side of my days at the trading company, and I don't usually talk about the "dark" side, because almost all my talks are recorded and they may leave deep impressions in listeners' minds. Many of the people I worked with at the trading company are still alive, and I don't want to cause them any trouble by talking about them.

The Seed for Significant Self-Growth Lies in Criticism

Now that I think about it, however, many of the difficulties I had with others, especially those who caused me distress and hurt me deeply, became nourishment for my soul later on. Today, I seldom receive direct criticism, but in those days I faced relentless censure, and I learned a lot from it.

It would take a lot of guts for someone to criticize me head-on today; even a head of state would be terrified to do so. If he made a negative remark about me—for example, "I despise Ryuho Okawa's facial expression"—and his comment were published in the newspaper, he would probably receive a flood of complaints from the members of our organization at his office, and so would the newspaper company, and all these complaints would be very difficult to handle. Even if I agreed with what he said about me, Happy Science members wouldn't forgive him so easily.

In any case, you may suffer from relationship issues at work, but if you do, it should help to know that not all the criticisms you receive are wrong. In fact, their criticisms are the seeds of drastic growth that can turn you into a more splendid person. What you need to do is to simply draw a lesson from the criticisms and use them to improve yourself. Even if you receive criticism from not-so-great people, their criticism can still be beneficial.

Democracy wouldn't work if we only received criticism from people who are more distinguished than ourselves. In a democracy, average citizens can elect or reject outstanding candidates for office. In other words, democracy functions on a couple of premises: first, even ordinary people can often point out the shortcomings, weaknesses, and failures of remarkable individuals, and second, we can see other people's characters as clear as a glass bowl, even if we are not aware of our own character.

So in a democratic society, the more distinguished you become, the more you will need to listen to criticism. As your social standing increases, what is acceptable for an ordinary person becomes unacceptable for you, and after a certain point, you will start facing censure even for a minor slip of the tongue. This experience can be quite painful, but in a sense, it shows how we need to bear the weight of responsibility that comes with high social standing. It's essential that we know this.

The more important a person you become, the more criticism you will receive. You will be criticized even for things that you previously weren't criticized about. Certain actions or behaviors are acceptable if you are a subordinate but unacceptable once you become a leader. Especially when a woman takes on a leadership position, she may hear things that she would not want anyone to point out. But this is inevitable when you are in the position of a leader. As your social standing goes up, you will inevitably receive complaints and criticisms from a variety of people.

Try Not to Take Harsh Criticism Personally

There are several things I have come to realize by experiencing criticism. One of them is particularly important for people with a religious disposition, because those who are pure of heart tend to take other's words too seriously and get hurt excessively. Those with a religious disposition often impose on themselves such precepts as not speaking ill of others. As a result, they become vulnerable to criticisms and verbal assaults, get deeply hurt, and allow the pain to linger for a long time.

I was like that when I was younger, but when I think back now, after a certain number of years, I came to realize that being too vulnerable and prolonging the hurt for a long time is a type of sin. Sometimes people say things without much thought. In many cases, they just say things that pop into their heads because of a certain situation or mood they were in. So you don't want to allow the pain of others' remarks to linger for ten or twenty years. The people who said the words that hurt your feelings probably had no intention of tormenting you for decades or making you suffer for a lifetime.

Of course, it sometimes happens that someone

has an intention to curse you for the rest of your life, targets you, and shoots an arrow of criticism at the best possible time to inflict pain for maximum effect. But that kind of thing will only happen once or twice in a lifetime, if that. Usually people don't think that far ahead or that deeply in their day-to-day lives. Most of us are ordinary people and not necessarily saints, which makes it inevitable that we sometimes get hurt by each other's remarks. But even if we take their words personally and find them offensive, we need to try to forget about them after one night's sleep, because many of the things people say are not well thought through.

For example, when you're criticized about your work or your company, you may suffer as a leader, but it could be that people are simply complaining because they want more attention. They can't take it when things don't go the way they want, and sometimes this feeling of frustration turns into attention-seeking behavior and comes out as criticism of their senior colleagues. We probably shouldn't ignore criticism completely, but neither should we take it too seriously. This is one of the important lessons I learned when I was younger. People of a religious disposition with a pure heart, in particular, can be very sensitive, so these people may need to learn to become a little tougher.

It helps to think about how you can equip yourself to defend yourself against the arrows of criticisms that come flying at you. If you observe aquatic creatures, for example, slimy fish such as catfish and eels have no scales on their bodies. Other types of fish do have scales, and other marine creatures such as turtles have shells on their backs. These creatures equip themselves differently to defend themselves.

In my case, although I do sometimes get hurt by criticism if what I said has been fundamentally misunderstood or has made anyone unhappy, I am no longer hurt by the common criticisms we receive every once in a while. This is because the level of the things I am worried about has risen to a higher dimension. My main concern now is how to bring happiness to many people, so little things no longer concern me.

Have the Fortitude to Let Go After One Night's Sleep

But this was not how I was when I was younger. In my student days, I even felt hurt when I found out that the girl I admired had gotten a higher score than mine. I was so devastated that I skipped dinner—I couldn't eat. It sounds silly now that I think about it. It was probably the very time I should have nourished myself and studied harder. That would have been the positive attitude that I should have adopted. I was simply naïve enough to be shocked into not being able to eat, just because the girl I admired had a higher score than mine.

If you get depressed about things like this every day, you'll perplex people around you and even prevent them from making an effort to do well. It wouldn't be right for them to study while thinking, "I don't want to hurt anyone's feelings, so I shouldn't study hard," or "I should hold myself back from achieving a good score, because I may offend others' pride." Your student days are a time of friendly competition. There are times when you do better than your friends in exams and other times when your friends do better than you, but from a larger perspective, these are like games you play and opportunities to improve yourself. So it's no good to hold a grudge about exam results. Especially those with a religious disposition should keep in mind that they shouldn't get hurt too easily or hold onto an emotional wound for too long. It's essential to know that doing so is a form of sin.

On the other hand, those who have hurt you may also feel bad that they've made a slip of the tongue and upset you. But even if they regret what they said, it's not always easy to apologize. Occasionally, they may find a chance to tell you they're sorry, but if they miss that chance, they may not have another one. In other words, seeing you get hurt can make them feel just as hurt. So it's essential to build a strong enough mind that you can forget what others have said to you after a good night's sleep. You will be able to develop that kind of inner fortitude if you make a conscious effort to do so.

Without scales, even fish cannot repel water. So first, we need to cover ourselves with a "skin" that will protect us from criticism. Next, we need to thicken our skin till it's as thick as the skin of the giant South American fish, the pirarucu. And to really protect ourselves, we need to make it as strong as a turtle's shell.

When you're working to achieve a big goal, obsessing and fretting over trifling matters only works against you.

The Higher Your Position Becomes, the Bigger Your Issues Become

In a sense, those who obsess over little things, get hurt, and cling to the hurt for a long time have a lot of time to kill. Hearing this may hurt them even more, but it's true. They have too much free time on their hands, which is why they can spend years and sometimes even decades distressed over what someone once said. Busy people simply can't afford to spend time on such trivial things.

For instance, a rank-and-file employee may anguish over and suffer from a reprimand he receives from his supervisor. But when a recession hits, the CEO of a big business with tens of thousands of employees has more serious issues to think about. The mental anguish you suffer from teetering on the brink of bankruptcy that would leave tens of thousands of employees jobless is on a completely different level from the pain you feel when someone scolds you. While most employees are often oblivious to the crisis the company is facing, executives usually know ahead of time that their company will collapse if it stays the way it is.

In fact, a certain Japanese airline was facing this kind of financial crisis around the time I delivered the lecture this chapter is based on. In January 2010, this airline filed a petition for protection under the Corporate Rehabilitation Law because it was expected that the airline's funds would fall short by ten billion yen at the end of the month. This meant that the company was on the verge of bankruptcy—of having its airplanes under lease seized, becoming unable to refuel, and having to withhold its employees' salaries. The airline had to quickly apply for protection under the Corporate Rehabilitation Law to avoid falling short of funds. You can probably imagine the suffering the executive managers had to go through. Naturally, they would have to resign, but they also found themselves in the difficult position of having to let go of one-third of their approximately fifty thousand employees. I am sure the management team at the time must have suffered many sleepless nights.

As we have seen, when you hold an important position, you no longer have room to think about each of the criticisms you receive or negative things others say about you. You have bigger issues to think about, and matters concerning a great number of people start to occupy your mind. When you look at the issues that trouble your mind right now from this perspective, you'll probably see how trivial they are compared to the kinds of problems that these top executives are struggling with.

Of course, I'm not telling you to completely ignore criticisms, accusations, and insults. If the criticism you receive is relevant in some respect, the most constructive way to deal with it is to use it for your self-growth. So one way to handle criticism is to see if it is valid and consider whether you can use it to improve yourself. Another way is to tell yourself not to be too sensitive to criticism and also not to hold onto the pain over a long period of time. It is actually a sin to let the hurt drag on for too long, and only those who have a lot of time to spare can afford to do so. Instead, use your time to think more constructive and positive thoughts, and you will no longer have time to obsess over such issues.

In fact, 99 percent of people worry, agonize, and fight over trifling and insignificant issues. Try for a moment to leave aside your own worries and observe the issues that others are struggling with from a bystander's perspective. You will probably be able to clearly see that many of the issues people struggle with aren't truly that important. People often get hurt over little things that happen at home, slight misunderstandings at work, and the casual remarks and actions of others.

When you realize that you've been distressed about trivial matters, you'll be able to treat them as such. Just as you throw away things you no longer need, you should not hold onto trivial hurts as if they're valuable treasures.

To sum up, I would like you to know that only 1 percent of the problems that trouble your mind are of real significance and require your careful consideration. The other 99 percent are often trifling matters that you don't have to agonize over.

2

Managing Financial Stress

Only Humans Suffer from the Lack of Money

The issues you struggle with are probably not limited to emotional or psychological ones, so let me talk about issues that involve other aspects of life. According to the questionnaire I mentioned earlier, besides relationship stress, quite a few people said they felt stressed about financial and economic hardships.

The distress of running short of money, or economic deprivation, is not a recent difficulty that only modern people face. People have been struggling with this issue for most of human history. In other words, there has almost never been a period when people's problem was that they had too much money.

Rather, 99 percent of the time, people lived from hand to mouth and were grateful if they had enough to eat for the day. Barely 1 percent of human history consists of abundant periods. So, I would like you to know that economic hardship can happen to anyone and is not a rare incident like a meteorite falling from space and hitting only you.

To begin with, economic hardship is unique to humans. As you know, wild animals do not make a single cent. In Japanese folklore, raccoons can turn leaves into fake money, but animals basically are not capable of economic activity. There are, of course, animals that work to help humans, such as guard dogs and guide dogs. But these dogs don't earn money for their work; all they get is perhaps some leftovers. The same goes for crows and dolphins: they're highly intelligent, but no company would employ them. So animals can neither work for a company nor take part in economic activity. On the other hand, most animals don't develop the complex illnesses that humans often get. People develop illness from stress caused by various factors. In fact, most modern diseases have mental causes.

Animals don't take medicine; they battle illness and injury only with their natural healing ability. They may feel stressed by cold, hunger, or the risk of being killed, but unlike humans, they don't develop complex diseases from stress. Animals don't get duodenal ulcers because of investment failures, suffer from gastric ulcers because their stock shares became worthless, or commit suicide because they lost a chance for promotion.

Animals are incapable of economic activity, but neither do they develop illnesses from mental anguish, go insane, or commit suicide. After all, physical ailments and malfunctions are often manifestations of events occurring in the inner world.

I Used Poverty as a Springboard to Develop a Self-Help Spirit

Most people are probably dissatisfied with their financial situation. I also suffered from a lack of money during my youth because my family was not very well off. My father's company went bankrupt around the time I was born, burdening him with debt for more than twenty years. This made our life extremely difficult financially, and I remember having an austere "money squeeze" because of this, but I don't think this was necessarily a bad thing.

I'm sure some people attribute their current financial difficulties to their economically disadvantaged parents. They may insist that this is evidenced by the fact that rich kids become rich, and some even become a prime minister. It is true that money can be an effective tool for getting some things done.

My parents were not like the mother of the former Japanese prime minister, who gave her son an allowance of more than one hundred thousand dollars every month. Rather, they would often remind me of the few hundred dollars they sent me every month for living expenses. But I never blamed my parents for my financial hardship. Instead I believed that becoming financially successful was up to me, and I was grateful to my parents for giving me the opportunity to give it a try.

From the age of twenty and onward, you have to get by with the knowledge, effort, and talents that you cultivate on your own. I'm now grateful for the financial difficulty of my youth, because it helped me develop a self-help spirit; it served as a driving force for diligent effort. I'm really glad that I didn't receive a one hundred thousand dollar allowance like the former prime minister of Japan. If I had, I would have lost the motivation to work.

In particular, when I was in college, I strongly felt that I had to work to support my family. At that time, my father was approaching the time to leave his job, and my family faced the prospect of going without an income because my older brother, who was enrolled in the philosophy department at Kyoto University, was loafing around without a job, pretending to be a philosopher. I knew that our family would face financial ruin unless I became financially stable, so I chose a job with a high salary. I resigned myself to this, in a sense, but it also became an important opportunity for success. I was able to turn the adversity into an opportunity.

For my part, I chose an occupation that would let me make the most of myself and offer me opportunities, but I received bitter criticism from those around me for this decision. Nonetheless, the company I joined taught me top leadership skills and gave me the chance to experience corporate executive training firsthand, albeit for a short time. The company probably never expected that I would leave, but the skills and experiences I acquired there became very useful when I left to found my religious organization.

At the trading company I worked for, it took a few decades for an average employee to grasp how the entire business operated. Entry-level employees were first trained to become specialists by being placed in a specific position, such as the steel business, condominium development, or orange importing from California, for about ten years. But unlike other employees, I was transferred to different divisions every year, because the company intended to train me to become an executive. This experience allowed me to learn about all aspects of the business in a short amount of time.

I am sincerely grateful to my parents for putting me in a financially difficult situation, because it gave me the motivation to work hard, which, as a result, gave me an opportunity for success. When I was still in college, I considered staying in academia to become a researcher, but I just couldn't see how I could earn a living that way, so I had no choice but to take a job with a good salary. Fortunately, that worked to my advantage, helping me run a religious organization now. Currently, our group is expanding on a global scale, and developing activities with a global vision and broadening the scope of work throughout the world are what I used to do when I was in the trading business. I feel that our organization is finally expanding the horizons of our activities to a similar level that the company I used to be a part of did.

Your Financial Situation Will Improve When You Strive to Benefit Others

Money doesn't fall from the sky. As I've repeatedly said in my books, such as *Prosperity Thinking**, you will receive some form of economic compensation for work that others find beneficial. This is how it works in this world, regardless of the industry you're in.

Put simply, what determines our income is not ourselves, but the people around us, our customers, and the general public. During difficult economic times, some companies prosper while others flounder, and even within the same company, some get raises and others don't. These things are determined not by the parties themselves, but by the people surrounding them.

So, you absolutely don't have to struggle desperately to make money. All you need to do is constantly strive to do work that helps many people. It's essential that you make it your joy to see the smiles

* Ryuho Okawa, *Prosperity Thinking* (Tokyo: HS Press, 2015).

and happiness of many people and see that joy as an extension of your work. It's impossible not to receive any financial reward for work that benefits others and is appreciated by many.

You may say that your products and services are excellent and should be selling better, but in the end their value will be assessed by your customers. I often hear people blaming the bad economy as a reason they went bankrupt, but they are simply making an excuse. Even among businesses on the same street or in the same area, some go under and others stay in business. And while some stores lose customers and go out of business, other stores increase their customer base under the same circumstances. You may not be able to help wondering why, but you need to humbly accept this fact.

With regard to economic issues, there is no need to think too deeply about specific, individual factors. As long as you are aiming to do a job that helps and benefits others, your economic situation will take a turn for the better regardless of where you work. If your present circumstances no longer let you fully use your abilities or talents, you'll soon find yourself opening a new chapter in life. This is how the world works.

People will recognize those who are performing jobs that benefit others, and they will come along and extend their helping hands at the most appropriate time and in the best possible way to give you a greater task. I'll say it again: there is no need to agonize too much over temporary financial issues. Do your work with a wish to benefit others, entrust the result to the divine, and pray. Then you will surely see a path opening up before you.

Recently, I've been offering a great many teachings at our organization about economic prosperity and management. This is probably why enterprises and companies run by Happy Science members have recently been introduced on TV and other media as businesses that have achieved remarkable sales growth. Despite the difficult economic times, some of them are outdoing their competitors with a bargain strategy, while others, conversely, are beating their rivals with a high-value-added strategy.

Many businesses are actually expanding amid the headwind of economic recession and boosting themselves by making full use of various strategies and tactics in the laws of management that I teach. Even in the business world, if your efforts to expand your company are driven by the high aspiration of helping change the world into a utopia, people will recognize your noble wish, and many collaborators will emerge among them. This is the kind of attitude I would like you to have.

3

How to Remove Worries about Old Age

I believe that many people are worried about aging. If asked what their greatest fear in life is, ultimately most people will say "death." The greatest fear of the living is death.

I have taught at length about the meaning of death and what happens after death, which means that if you have read my books, you are already free from most people's greatest fear. Learning the Truths will enable you to conquer the fear of death and the terror of suffering in hell after death. If you are familiar with Happy Science teachings, you already know how to conquer these fears. Happy Science offers measures to combat this greatest fear. And if death is your biggest fear in life, then everything else becomes a smaller fear, so if you can overcome your fear of death, you can overcome all fear.

Some of you reading this may be worried about the hardships you may suffer in your old age because perhaps you have few relatives and you have no prospect of receiving financial support. You may even imagine yourself left virtually homeless and dying a painful death without having been able to receive treatment for your illness. But there is no need to anguish over these thoughts.

If you have strong faith and pray for a healthy and active life until the end and to have a painless death, God will take you at the right time. When heaven decides that it's better for you not to remain on Earth for long and that the time has come for you to come back, you will pass away smoothly at the right time. You will be able to die without having to worry about a lack of money. All you need to leave behind is enough money to cover your funeral expenses. Even if you are short of funds, it will work out in the end if everyone chips in.

So please don't worry too much about suffering the pain of old age by living for a long time. If you're still worried, you can join a club we have at Happy Science called "Society for Living to 100," where you can make good friends with whom you can study the teachings of the Truths. These friends will help you if something happens to you. When you become a member of our group, you will no longer have to worry so much about old age.

4

Keys to Freeing Your Mind from Stress

Awakening to the Fact that Your Life Is Priceless

There are many people out there who say that they don't own anything—neither money nor property nor assets. But in fact, everyone has lots of things. For example, relationships with others are one such thing. As I discussed earlier, certain types of relationships can become a source of worry, but I'm sure you have many other types of relationships that can help you.

Also, we can certainly be grateful for having a body of our own. Organ transplants have become a common practice nowadays. Some parents in impoverished parts of developing nations are selling their children's kidneys, eyes, and other body parts to survive.

In other cases, parents cut off one of their children's arms so that they can live on as a beggar.

It's a blessing to be able to walk on our own legs, eat with our own hands, and work. What do you think would happen if we asked people in affluent countries like Japan and America to sell their arms? How much do you think they would be willing to sell them for? Would you sell one of your arms for one million dollars and both of your arms for two million dollars, or two arms and two legs for a total of four million dollars? Probably not. This means that your arms and legs are actually worth more than that. And if you were asked to sell your right eye or your brain, how much would you sell it for? I doubt you would ever want to sell it, no matter how much money you were offered. You would simply refuse to sell your eye or brain.

As a side note, when medical science advances further, we may be able to replace our brain one day. The time may come when we can remove an impaired part of our brain and replace it with an intelligent person's brain to improve our memory. This kind of brain transplant may become popular among people who need to take exams. Considering the progress medical technology is making today, this might happen within a generation. Wealthy parents who performed poorly in school may believe that their children were born unintelligent and may wish to have their children's brains replaced with the brains of children born to intelligent parents. Even if such a thing becomes possible however, I don't think anyone would be willing to sell their brain, no matter how much they were offered, because it is priceless.

The point is that we are all living a priceless life, and we are actually blessed with a lot of things. Air is indispensable to all living creatures, and we can breathe it for free. Imagine how awful it would be if you were told to pay for the oxygen you breathe over the course of your lifetime. It would be terrible, for example, if the government introduced an "oxygen tax" because they needed revenue. If the government claimed that the oxygen in the country's territory belongs to the country, citizens would be stuck paying a tax to the government for the oxygen they breathe within the country's territory (although if such a tax bill were passed, no one would stay in such a country). Sunlight is also free. We don't have to pay a certain amount per hour for exposure to the sun's rays. I ask you to please remember that humans are already given the essentials of life for free.

Instead of Thinking Only about Yourself, Wish for the Happiness of Others

Humans have the duty to live happily or to strive to live a happy life. But if you want to live happily, you need to wish for the happiness of many others. When you do this, you will become happy. It's hard to find happiness when you are only seeking your own happiness. It's when you try to bring happiness to others that you find happiness for yourself. Strangely enough, those who worry about themselves can't become happy. You can probably see this when you observe others. Those who are constantly worried about themselves—grumbling, complaining, criticizing others, or picking on others' faults—don't look happy.

These people are not happy because they see things from a self-centered perspective. Conversely, those who don't think much about themselves but instead busy themselves with looking after and caring about others often find themselves happy. Put simply, those who spend a lot of time holding negative thoughts or worrying about themselves are not very happy. The more time you devote to others—whether through your company, your religious organization, or other activities—and the more you realize that you almost didn't think about yourself all day, the more moments of happiness you'll experience.

Occupy Yourself with Work and Finish Your Work Quickly

A proper break is necessary to de-stress. We also asked in the questionnaire how people relieve stress, and the answers included sleeping, getting a massage, having a big meal, and drinking a moderate amount of alcohol. These common methods for de-stressing are generally effective. Getting rest is another effective way to relieve stress, so taking a proper rest every now and then is also important.

To stop worrying about the little things, it's also essential to stay busy and make sure you have things to do all the time. For instance, if you focus your mind on things you have to do tomorrow and occupy yourself by preparing for them, you won't have time to worry about other things. It's important to keep ourselves busy, because issues that trouble our mind often seem to grow bigger when we have a lot of time on our hands.

However, if you are suffering from too much work, you probably need to learn to make quick decisions so you can complete your tasks quickly. Doing this will enable you to decrease your workload and free up your time so you can be ready to take on a new job at any time. This will not only open a path to promotion, but also eliminate your worries. In general, when you have to handle more than one job at a time, you'll be torn between conflicting demands, so my advice is to finish your work quickly. I hope that by practicing these methods of relieving stress, you'll be able to sleep deeply and peacefully all night.

CHAPTER TWO

improving your relationships

1

Everyone Has a Different Perception and Understanding of Things

Relationship issues can cause us a lot of stress, and perhaps you are in search of the solution to your own relationship problem. I wish I could speak to your problem individually, since everyone's problems are different and everyone has unique needs.
But in this chapter, I would like to give general, universal advice on how to improve our relationships so that my teachings can benefit many people.

The first thing we need to understand is that our problems in relationships have to do with the nature of people's perceptions. No one's perceptions are exactly the same as another's. Each one of us views things differently, and this is the root of all our problems in human relationships.

Let me share a story that will illustrate what this means:

A specialist in the United States who was working with recovering alcoholics once made this demonstration in a seminar. He prepared two glasses, one filled with water and the other filled with highly concentrated alcohol. Then he took out a worm. First he placed the worm inside the glass of water, and the worm crawled out full of energy. Then he placed the same worm inside the glass filled with alcohol, and moments later, it had died.

The specialist intended for this demonstration to show the harmful effects of drinking alcohol—to show that it is destructive enough to kill a living organism in an instant. But when the specialist asked the audience to share their thoughts and what they had learned from his demonstration, one audience member, to the specialist's great dismay, responded, "Now I know that drinking alcohol can help kill the bugs in my stomach."

Certainly, this is one possible way of understanding this experiment.

I guess if alcohol is capable of killing a worm, it may also help kill the bugs in our stomachs and disinfect our intestines. Still, I'm sure that the specialist was dumbstruck by this reaction, which illustrates that individual differences in perceptions give rise to issues in human relationships and that perceptions can differ widely from person to person, even when referring to the same thing.

People who particularly cause relationship stress are the egocentric type—people who take a self-centered perspective. This may indeed be the hardest type of person to have a harmonious relationship with. Like the alcoholic patient from the funny story I just told, other people won't always understand your goodwill and true intentions. If you were one of the members of Happy Science, you would often try to introduce your friends to your faith with the best of intentions. But perhaps some would mistakenly perceive Happy Science to be an untrustworthy religion and feel victimized. There are times like this in life, when differences in perceptions inevitably affect our current relationships.

We need to accept the fact that people perceive things differently. Understanding that others' perceptions and understandings can differ allows our own awareness of the world to enlarge and helps us gain open-mindedness and tolerance toward others and the diverse ways that people can think. If we strongly believe that our own perspective is the only possible one, it makes improving our relationships difficult to do.

2

Find Others' Strengths

Looking at People's Strong Points Avoids Making Them Your Enemies

To find the course that will take you smoothly through this life in a positive direction, it's important to look at others' strong points and positive aspects. Focusing on others' strengths will allow you to avoid making them your enemies; they will think nicely of you and see you as someone they want to befriend and develop a relationship with.

In contrast, if you give others the sense that you're always pointing out others' flaws, you will make them want to avoid you in the end. Even when you are in the right and this is a fact they are aware of, they will want to keep their distance from you anyway.

For this reason, developing a habit of seeing the strengths in others as much as you can will help you improve your relationships and make more friends. Clearly resolving to make this practice one of your life principles will make it possible to do this more easily than you might expect. The first step is to wish to cultivate this habit. And when you do, it will begin to unfold into reality before you.

I want to repeat again how important it is to strive to recognize other people's good points to improve your relationships. It's important to look for the strengths in each of the people you meet in the course of life and strive to look at this side of them all the time.

We should take caution about one thing, however. While studying a lot for school can develop your attention to detail, it can also give you a tendency to look out for "trick questions," causing you to be very perceptive of others' flaws and shortcomings. Put differently, becoming "smarter" can also make you keenly discerning of people's weaknesses, and this can be a dangerous trap in your mind.

Of course, a managerial or leadership position requires that we recognize people's shortcomings and weaknesses. A blind eye turned to the flaws of our subordinates and associates can impede our ability to fulfill our responsibilities. Good leaders will recognize people's shortcomings, but will still want to help them develop and cultivate their strengths. So, as managers and leaders, we shouldn't remain oblivious to others' faults and weaknesses. But we need to be mindful that growing smarter can also mean growing keener and scrutinizing about people's weaknesses and negative aspects, leading us to be disliked. This is something we don't usually recognize about ourselves unless someone else notices and tells us. Many people suffer from this tendency especially in their younger days.

The more that our thinking grows precise and in mathematical and scientific ways, the better we get at noticing small mistakes, flaws, and weaknesses in other people. It makes it difficult to develop friendships with people who have this tendency. If this is a trait that we, ourselves, have, we want to start thinking in this way instead: "I am also sometimes wrong and do make mistakes. And when I do, I feel very blessed when others treat me forgivingly and acceptingly, so other people must feel the same way when they make mistakes."

An Experience of Human Relationships in My Own Life

In my early working days, I had an experience with a friend that relates to what I have just discussed. Like me, my friend was an alumnus of the University of Tokyo, and since he was good at speaking English, he often attended an English conversation session that took place over coffee on his days off. At the time, there was a coffee shop located around Ebisu in Tokyo where customers spoke only English. He regularly went to this coffee shop because it allowed him to have conversations in English for long hours at a very low price.

One day my friend invited me to join him. I would have rather declined to go, but he somehow coerced me into going and introduced me to his girlfriend, whom he had actually met at the same coffee shop. They were already engaged and had plans to get married soon.

My friend introduced me to her as his best friend, and the three of us started chatting. But when my friend left for the restroom, his fiancée asked me a question: "I heard that you are his best friend, and I wish I could find out about all his strengths and weaknesses before our wedding. Can you tell me about his flaws? Other people have told me about his good points, but no one has told me about his weaknesses yet. As his best friend, you must know a lot about them and I was hoping you'd share them with me."

My personality has been straightforward ever since I was a child. In other words, I always spoke very frankly because I believed it would be wrong not to practice honesty or to lie if someone wanted to know the truth, so I gave her my honest opinion of my friend's flaws.

I told her, "First, there's his habit of interrupting others mid-conversation. This is a bad habit of his that he should try to break. Second, he lacks vitality. It's not so ideal for him to get so tired and exhausted so easily, so he needs more physical strength. He also has a habit of excessive drinking and likes to go out to drink every night. I think he'll continue this habit even in marriage and may not come home on some nights. So, you should try to help him with his drinking habit." She listened earnestly and nodded her head as I explained these things to her.

But after I'd left, she told my friend to stop being friends with a person like me and to end our friendship. She was surprised and said to him that I'd spoken ill of him when I was supposed to be his best friend, and she told him that she wouldn't be able to forgive me for what I'd said. Her reaction took me completely by surprise, because I hadn't realized that what I had said would make her feel that way.

Point Out Others' Flaws in a Positive Way

When I explained to my friend what had happened, he gave me this advice: "When telling someone else about your best friend's flaws, you're supposed to describe them as if they are his strengths." He has a good point. For example, instead of saying, "He has an excessive drinking habit and drinks every night," I should have told her, "He is too sociable." By saying, "Having a sociable personality is one of his weaknesses," I make him sound like a nice person. Also, instead of saying, "He often interrupts people's conversations," I could have rephrased it to say, "His conversational skills are very advanced. Just as he is good at speaking English, he is very good at holding conversations." Furthermore, when I said, "His lack of vitality makes him get tired and exhausted very easily," I should have added, "This is because of his excellent concentration skills."

Because I was asked to point out his faults, I

responded straightforwardly. But this angered his fiancée to the point that she told my friend not to see me anymore. I remember how awful this incident made me feel.

In short, being honest doesn't necessarily lead to relationship success. All relationships in the world require some kind of "cushioning." Especially when meeting someone for the first time or in a situation like the one I was in, you need to prepare a bit of "cushioning" while thinking about what the other person is seeking from the conversation. This experience helped me learn that I should not always take what other people say at face value.

I was very quick-witted in my youth, so I had no difficulty pointing out others' faults or mistakes. But this experience with my best friend taught me that this ability was no longer something I wanted to be proud of.

It's better to practice some vagueness when describing someone else's faults and shortcomings. It's better to seem unaware of their flaws when you're talking to them, as if you haven't noticed anything, even if you really have. At the same time, it's good to show recognition of their strengths by saying, "Such and such is a great thing about you." Doing so can work positively in your relationships, and my understanding of this developed over time.

When young people stumble in their relationships, it's usually a result of speaking too directly about other people's flaws. They just need to practice more caution and consideration toward others. Speaking badly of someone may bring feelings of regret soon afterward and may make you feel bad about what you've done, but it's not always because of a bad personality. Your ability to spot these flaws may be a sign of a quickwitted mind and an ability to analyze people. From a higher perspective, it's easy to notice what's lacking in others.

To avoid rifts in your relationship, be careful about the time, situation, and who you are talking to. The best thing you can do to improve your relationships is make the effort to look for others' strengths. Carefully observe their strengths, and glance lightly over their weaknesses. It's better to be aware of their weaknesses than unaware, but you can make an effort to see them in a carefree manner.

Mistakes to Avoid When Offering Praise

Taking this a step further, I would like to add that it's important to compliment others' strengths, but doing so with an intention to take advantage of them will ruin the relationship in the end, even if it seems to go smoothly in the beginning.

Compliments may flatter and delight others and strengthen their feelings of friendship toward you. But praise based on desires for self-gain will ultimately drive your relationship toward a great downfall. Compliments shouldn't issue from an intention to lie or deceive or to gain people's favor. When members of a notorious new religion approach people, they often start with a compliment, but occasionally lies are hidden behind their words. They use praise to persuade you to join their religion, but sometime down the road, their true intentions are revealed.

A hidden agenda or desire to take advantage of others will inevitably lead to a failed relationship, so we need to be mindful of our intentions. Even if our compliments draw their attention at first, sooner or later they are bound to realize, "This person just wanted to use me," and stop trusting us. We need to be careful of the way we compliment others.

Praise must come from your heart. It's important not to overdo your praise. Otherwise, it will make people think, "I received so many compliments when we first met, but now I am treated so differently. What's going on?" And your relationship may turn sour. We mustn't give superficial compliments; instead we must speak from our hearts without any thoughts about taking advantage of others. This is one of the ways to build good relationships.

3

Give Each Other Space

How to Get Along with an Egocentric Person

Those who cause headaches in relationships may be very similar to the alcoholic I talked about earlier who concluded that alcohol helps get rid of bugs in our stomachs—he represents the egocentric type who may be the hardest type of person to deal with and also a difficult type to avoid. Their perceptions have become so hardened that it feels almost impossible to change their way of thinking. Pride overfills them, making them difficult to deal with unless they're allowed to realize their mistakes on their own.

People who accept their mistakes when they're pointed out to them aren't egocentric in the first place. Egocentrics are the people who have a twisted perspective of things. It's hard for them to admit that they have been wrong when mistakes are pointed out too directly. They need others to warn them about their errors in an indirect way.

To put this another way, egocentrics feel no qualms about changing their thoughts and views when they discover their own mistakes. What we can do, then, to avoid hurting anyone's feelings, is help them see, on their own, that their actions may lead to undesirable outcomes.

What may ruin your relationship with this type, however, is forcing them to apologize and promise to never make the same mistake again, as you would do when admonishing a small child. This kind of rebuke may tempt very prideful people to act out. I think the better approach, then, is to offer indirect hints about the mistake and do your best to foster feelings of self-reproof. This may be a very sophisticated approach, but it is actually necessary when it comes to working out your relationships with very proud people.

Guard Your Inner Space from Overly Aggressive People

It's not just the twisted perceptions of egocentric people that make them hard to deal with; it's also their attempts to force their views on you. For example, the alcoholic patient who misinterpreted the specialist's demonstration might go around to his friends and acquaintances and recommending that they drink alcohol every day to cleanse their stomachs. Dealing with unwanted pressure to accept other people's views like this is another problem we face in human relationships.

When you're placed under pressure to accept someone else's fixed opinion, without consideration for your own, it is important to guard your inner space from them or set down certain boundaries. Relationships often go more smoothly when both sides respect each other's independence and give each other the personal space they deserve. Relationships end quickly when one side becomes completely dependent on the other or one tries to completely "defeat" the other.

In a common kind of comedy duo in Japan, one comedian always plays the role of the fool and the other always corrects the partner's mistakes. As a comedy performance, this can be entertaining. But in a real-world situation, this kind of relationship is bound to be short-lived.

If you're in a distressing relationship where you often feel forced to accept the other person's views, it's important to guard yourself against that pressure to some degree. Think in your heart, "I will let in this person's views, but only to a certain degree. Beyond that point is where my own personal space lies; it's my sacred territory. No one else is allowed to change or control this space of mine." Guarding your own inner space from intrusion is essential, and as long as you protect this space, you'll feel more comfortable when exchanging opinions about other topics.

Mutual independence and respect for one another's inner space are keys to lasting relationships. So we need to decide how we want to associate with other people depending on how hardened their ideas and perceptions are.

Avoid Encroaching on Other People's Spaces

The hospitable people of the Japanese countryside warmly welcome outside visitors into their homes. But when we travel to these places, we don't want to accept their invitations at face value. If we do, we may be surprised when we find them talking to others, in secret, about how bold our manners are. An unspoken understanding exists in these areas that people from out of town may not know about. Those who don't know these customs take their hospitality more straightforwardly than it's intended.

You might happily accept their invitation to lunch and gladly agree to stay for dinner as well, only to discover later that staying for two meals was considered very bold manners. Finding the right measure of closeness is essential because of these kinds of situations.

In Kyoto, asking your guests if they would like to have some *ochazuke*—green tea poured over rice—is their polite way of asking their guests to take their leave. Not being familiar with this gesture may tempt us to stay and have some. The thought of tasting the well-known pickled vegetables of Kyoto that often come with ochazuke may be especially tempting, and we may easily stumble into making this mistake.

This roundabout manner of speaking to each other is characteristic of the people of Kyoto. Being delicately mannered, not a word of complaint will be spilled in front of you, and they may even converse with you, saying, "Aren't these pickled vegetables delicious?" "This tea is made from the famous tea leaves of the Uji region." But don't let this confuse you. When they ask, "Would you like to stay and have some ochazuke?" remember that this is a kindly meant sign that it is time for you to leave. Just politely respond, "Thank you, but it's time for me to get going soon," and leave. This is what we really need to do, but knowing how to act properly in this kind of social situation can be difficult.

4

Summing Up—Three Keys to Improving Relationships

Understanding that Perceptions Vary

Let me review what I have discussed so far in this chapter. The first, basic aspect of building smooth relationships is to understand that there are individual differences in perceptions and ways of thinking. When we assume that others see things the way we do and think the way we think, we breed discord in our relationships. But gaining awareness of other people's different views and perspectives allows us to cultivate open-mindedness and a big heart.

Seeing Others' Strong Points

The second point I raised was about striving to

recognize other people's good points and strengths instead of their faults and weaknesses. Pointing out people's flaws and shortcomings to prove our own intelligence is not what we want to do. You'll find yourself being able to do these things by resolving in your heart to do so.

If you are in a managerial position or other position of influence, completely disregarding others' faults and weaknesses can make it hard to meet your responsibilities. In this case, it's necessary to be aware of others' shortcomings. But when you call others' attention to their weaknesses, it's best to do so indirectly. By allowing them to believe that they identified their mistakes on their own, you keep from hurting their feelings. Giving severe rebukes and forceful reprimands would be like treating them like children and can rupture your relationships. But by noticing people's good points and putting their strengths to use, you'll create smooth relationships.

I should add to this that rifts may occur between the people you praise. You can handle this by setting your priorities carefully. If you find that a particular employee has the best ideas for a certain project, make that person the leader. Consider each project carefully, and determine whose strengths are best suited to each one.

Acknowledging One Another as Individuals and Being Considerate of One Another's Space

The third point I discussed was about having respect for each other as individuals, as unique and independent people. This mutual acknowledgement is vital to cultivating smooth relationships. It's important to respect the independent thinking and inner space of those you know.

5

Cultivate the Heart that Blesses the Successful

"Crabs Inside a Bucket"—Japanese Societies of Egalitarian Values

Up to now, I have talked about how relationships can be improved by people in general, and now there are some thoughts I would like to add about a common issue I have seen arising in relationships among Japanese people. Egalitarian values have long been established in Japan, and their roots can be found in agricultural societies. In such societies, people who stand out from among others tend to be disliked. These societies favor people who can live like others and harmonize with them. This is the philosophy that Japanese civilization originally began with. It is a country that began with sentiments that disfavored those who were different and exceptional enough to leave the small community and succeed.

This is why Japanese people have often been compared to crabs in a bucket. The crabs try to escape, but when one of them gets to the top, another one reaches up with its claws and pulls it down. Another crab may make the same attempt at success only to have the same thing happen.

There are many people who wish to go out into the world and succeed, but when success eludes them, they can't stand to see others succeed, so they try to bring them down. As a result, no one ends up becoming successful. If only they could all join their efforts together, many of them would find success, but they never try. This is a characteristic of agricultural-based societies.

The basis of this way of thinking comes from the long-established belief that the bounty of a harvest is influenced not by individual effort or capability, but by Mother Nature's blessings. This belief is why being exceptional or having a chance to move on from the life they all share is so frowned upon, and why people who strive for these things are forced down. This is a reality of the agricultural societies around Japan.

In a sense, this perspective on equality is a developed form of jealousy that has hardened. Put another way, a society that doesn't allow people to be different from one another turns jealousy into a vile desire for equality.

In this age of tremendous change, however, even these regions of the countryside will need to free themselves from this culture. Instead of stopping people from getting out and taking flight into the world, they should offer support to lift these people up. These people will then be able to help others escape from the bucket, one by one, until everyone is freed from the world of their "bucket." This is the heavenly perspective with which I feel we should look at things. Thinking about how we can lift each and every person up, rather than dragging them down, is a mindset that leads to blessing others' success.

The analogy of the crabs in a bucket actually refers to Japanese descendants in Hawaii, and the trait it describes has also been recognized in Brazilians of Japanese descent. This means that even Japanese people who live in another country have perpetuated the culture of pulling down those who stand out. Indeed, Japanese genetics must be incredibly resilient!

This trait seems to persist among the Japanese descendants, even if they speak another language and live in a foreign country.

I still remember when I read a book about the Japanese emigrants, and I came to realize that Japanese people have this characteristic. This analogy helped open my eyes at some point in my youth.

The Heart that Blesses the Successful Leads to Your Own Success

With a culture that supports the successful and helps others succeed, the number of successful people will grow and the society as a whole will be enriched.

I would like to add a word of advice for those who face issues with human relationships because of the culture of the crabs who drag others down. Now, in these very changeful times, it serves us better to cultivate a heart of blessing that pays recognition to those who succeed in the world. Those whom you bless will in turn reach out a helping hand to you in the future. Or perhaps those who leave your hometown to find success elsewhere may return your goodwill in the form of contributions to your hometown. If you find within yourself a tendency to speak badly of those who have succeeded, you need to rethink this mindset and change it.

What I have just explained is something that all people of Japan and Japanese cultures can learn from. The mindset of dragging down the successful is a trait that can be found across Japan, including in rural societies and lawmakers. It's a custom of trying to avoid the outstanding from receiving the recognition they deserve.

If you truly desire to enrich your country and foster true greatness, you must not forget to cultivate a heart of blessing. The idea of a heart of blessing may sound Christian, and I believe that this heart is somewhat lacking among the Japanese people. So I would like for everyone to know that the successful are those who have been blessed by the grace of God, and by blessing such people, you allow yourself to receive God's grace too.

CHAPTER THREE

a heart of blessing

1 Speaking Badly of Others Leads to Unhappiness

The Close Relationship between the Heart of Blessing and My Enlightenment

In this chapter, I would like to talk about the heart of blessing, which is deeply related to the enlightenment I attained in my youth. Blessing is an act of congratulating other people or praying for their happiness. This word has a rather Christian ring to it, but I would like to use the word "blessing" to also refer to the heart of praise.

The word "blessing" also means a lot to me personally. When I was younger, I was very vulnerable and had the sensitive heart of a poet. I used to get easily hurt by others' words and also keenly felt other people's pain, and these things would often torment and distress my heart. "A heart of blessing" is one of the phrases I encountered at that time.

The Positive and Negative Aspects of a Competitive Society

As you know, today's society has become highly competitive. From a larger perspective, competition is a principle that helps people strive to improve. In other words, it guides people to aim for growth and the attainment of happiness. So we can affirm it as a social system in which many people compete with one another in many aspects of life, including school, sports, work, and earnings. If there were no competition in society, it would be more likely for corruption and decline to occur, which would cause the society to stagnate and inhibit the evolution of souls. So, overall, I think a competitive society is beneficial to humanity because it can bring out the strengths of many people.

But in reality, living in a competitive society means that we often go through things that hurt us, create setbacks, and make us feel insecure, miserable, and helpless. Children and adults alike constantly find themselves in competition. But the consequence is that, society has evolved compared with one or two generations ago, and the overall level of happiness seems to have increased, so from a broader perspective, I think we can acknowledge that this is a positive system. Nevertheless, some aspects of this system can work negatively at the individual level, so that's where the system needs to improve.

The Badmouthing Trend Is Strongly Influenced by Mass Media

In today's society in particular, there is a trend of targeting certain people for public execution by criticism and bad-mouthing. Television has played an influential role in creating this trend. If you listen to what popular entertainers and comedians say on TV shows, many of them bash, criticize, and disparage others as a way to get laughs from the audience. This type of joke appears to be mainstream now, and regardless of who the entertainer is, they all seem to generally go with the same pattern of trying to make the audience laugh by finding fault with and mocking certain people.

Doing this allows both the celebrity and the audience to vent their frustrations and let out stress, which is often what people need to do. This serves as part of the "bread and circuses" approach to appeasing public discontent. The celebrity often puts on a "circus" or entertainment designed to make people feel better by using harsh words to "behead" people. I would like to refrain from mentioning the names of any specific celebrities here, but many entertainers do this to get laughs, become popular, and earn a favorable reputation.

This kind of trend is widespread in today's society. Children who watch these shows on TV accept and mimic these actions. At school, they speak badly of their friends and disparage others, engage in name-calling battles, and drag each other down, because they find these behaviors funny or amusing. As a consequence, children who speak politely and courteously and refrain from badmouthing others are treated as "weirdos" and often become the targets of attacks, slander, and bullying. To defend themselves, these children would have to fight back against the abusive language by hurling even harsher words at their attackers.

The same principle is at work in relationships between students and teachers. Such violent behaviors as attacking teachers, obstructing classes, and creating classroom chaos have become rampant in schools. In fact, these incidents mostly result from disruptive language and behavior.

It won't be easy to reverse this trend, because many people think this behavior is acceptable or even "cool." Even relatively more hardline, conservative newspapers and TV shows use the mainstream approach of accusing or criticizing people. This tendency can be beneficial when it's used to oust those who lie, deceive, and commit wrongdoings and to keep away evil and challenge injustice.

In fact, condemnation is related to the beginning of democracy in the modern world. The era of democracy began with the use of condemnation as a way of driving out tyrannical or corrupt kings and emperors, so we cannot reject condemnation completely. On the contrary, valid criticism is often necessary. Nevertheless, I doubt that spreading and affirming badmouthing is a fundamentally good practice.

Badmouthing Is Proof of Unhappiness

People who always speak ill of others are not happy.

You can probably see this when you observe them. When we're filled with happiness, we simply can't keep on saying bad things about others. So badmouthing is proof that we're unhappy. Someone who has a habit of criticizing others up front, making derogatory remarks as soon as he finds something he can belittle, or directly expressing jealousy, envy, and resentment is, simply, not a happy person.

These people are often trapped in a vicious cycle: they badmouth others because they're unhappy, and speaking ill of others makes them even more miserable. And they won't be able to find happiness until they correct this tendency. You will understand why their badmouthing makes them unhappier if you imagine yourself as their friend. You probably prefer to make friends with people who offer you compliments and would rather not become friends with people who openly make derogatory remarks about you. You would need considerable resilience, patience, and tolerance to stay friends with such people for a long time, and it would be a difficult path.

Perhaps when we are young, we might form a playful relationship that involves teasing each other. But as we pass a certain stage in adulthood, fewer and fewer people will accept our badmouthing as a joke, so it becomes increasingly difficult to form normal adult friendships.

Human beings want to become friends with people who compliment us, not people who talk negatively about us. So those who insult others all the time are basically saying that they don't want to be anyone's friend. Badmouthing is like a blatant refusal to be a good friend.

It would certainly be sad and lonely to be this way. And even if the person wants to stop this habit, they won't be able to change it overnight, especially if they're in their teens or early twenties.

Subjective and Self-Centered Views Prompt Derogatory Remarks

But what makes people speak badly of others in the first place? Why do people say hideous, resentful, and angry things to others? If we examine ourselves, we will find that we often say negative things when we're extremely hurt. Of course, we get hurt when others become angry with us, put us down, or disparage us. But we also feel crushed when we don't receive compliments and even when we see others getting praise.

Young people are especially self-centered in this respect. They often cannot assess their situation objectively and tend to think and act based on their feelings or their subjective and self-centered views. And from the perspective of full-fledged adults, young people seem extremely egoistic, and in fact, most young people are this way, although there are some exceptions.

But young people see their self-centeredness as purity. They often glamorize themselves, thinking that they say harsh and derogatory things to others only because they are pure and honest to themselves. As a result, they lose their friends or become isolated and feel increasingly lonely and sad. On top of that, it's not likely for a lot of good things to happen to these kinds of people, and that will drive them to alienate themselves further and feel even more desperately alone and tormented.

Furthermore, people with this negative tendency of denying others often find it difficult to accept the good things that do happen to them and deny them instead. Even if something positive happens to them, they refuse to accept it, thinking, "There must be something more going on than meets the eye," "This is only temporary, and I'll be let down later," "This might be some sort of trap," "Someone might be pulling my leg," or "This sort of thing just doesn't happen to me. So I won't believe it unless the same thing happens many times. I won't believe a one-time thing." They harbor thoughts that lead them toward unhappiness, and they end up developing a delicate and gloomy personality. These people often create a vicious circle of hurting others and causing them misery, which comes back to them and brings them more unhappiness. They end up creating a small and very dark world for themselves.

One of the underlying causes of this behavior is, as I mentioned earlier, the fact that the modern society is very competitive and creates winners and losers in various situations. But even in a completely equal society where there was no winning or losing, there would still be social exclusion, because people often reject those who are even slightly different in some way. This happens not only in the business community where corporations compete with one another, but also in agricultural village communities, where people sometimes try to drag down those who rise above others in the village and ostracize those who are below average.

In other words, whether in free, competitive societies or equal, non-competitive societies, people apply a similar principle to those who are different from others. This principle of excluding different types of people seems to be at work both when freedom is the governing principle and when equality is the guiding value.

You've probably heard of the motto, "Liberty, equality, and fraternity (fellowship)." As a matter of fact, although the ideas of liberty and equality can benefit a certain group of people, they could also be used to ostracize, persecute, and expel others. That's why we need to cultivate a generous heart: so we will cherish and become friends with a broad range of people. In this respect, it's essential to know that the principle of love creates harmony among people.

The Way You Think Has the Power to Change You

I had known the word "blessing" for quite some time, but it wasn't until around age twenty that I considered it in relation to myself, contemplated it, embraced it, and decided to change the way I lived and thought.

Consequently, I was able to change myself considerably, and based on my own experience, I realized how our thoughts have the power to change us.

Some of you may say that your tendency to speak negatively about others is a temperament that you genetically inherited from your parents and that you're born with it, or that it's a cultural attribute that you acquired by growing up in a society where it was common. Certainly, each of us is profoundly affected by our family, school, community, and other circumstances as we build our character during the first twenty years of our life.

But I experienced that people can change if they change the way they think and this is how I came to realize that thoughts have power. This realization became a basic principle of my work. Now, as a religious leader, my main job is to give lectures on the Truths, but if my lectures don't have the power to influence people, they'll be fruitless no matter how many I deliver.

I was able to change myself when I understood and accepted the heart of blessing others and tried to change my way of thinking—perhaps not completely, but I was able to at least recognize that I had changed, which made me believe that the same change could happen to others, too.

In Buddhism, these experiences are a type of enlightenment or, in other words, they are words of wisdom that open your eyes and guide you through life. You don't know the power of these words until you become aware of them, but once you do, they can turn you into a completely different person and give you a new life. This experience had a huge impact on me.

2

Feelings of Unhappiness Come from Comparing Yourself with Others

It's Easy to Get Jealous, but It Takes Effort to Bless Others

Vulnerable people often cannot imagine becoming happy, so they try to relieve their unhappiness by making other people feel unhappy. But this just keeps them stuck in a quagmire of their own making. What these people need to realize is that their unhappiness is rooted in their tendency to compare themselves with others.

Of course, it's impossible for us to be exactly the same as everyone else. Some people are superior to others in some ways. And we may sometimes find ourselves at the bottom when others are at their peak or riding a wave of success. Due to a range of factors, including timing, ability, and circumstances, some people's talents bloom at a certain point and they can savor the joy of happiness and success. And feeling jealous of their success is probably an instinctive reaction.

Basically, we can feel jealous without trying. Strangely enough, we know how to be jealous, even if we were never taught how. Toddlers are jealous of their slightly older or younger siblings when their parents treat them differently. Jealousy is a feeling everyone can experience instinctively without being taught or having to learn how.

In contrast, we have to want to cultivate a heart of blessing, whether by learning from others or by figuring it out on our own. Unlike jealousy, which we can harbor naturally, we need to learn how to cultivate a heart of blessing that congratulates others' successes or prays for their happiness. We don't understand the idea of blessing and its significance unless we learn to acquire a heart of blessing.

Christianity teaches blessing others as one of its doctrines, but even if we're not Christians, we can learn blessing as a moral teaching from our families, teachers, or friends.

Those who have been deeply hurt and have consequently developed a tendency to speak ill of others may at first think it's hypocritical to "bless" others. To them, congratulations sound like empty and superficial words coming from someone with a dark heart. But it's not hypocritical to bless others, and it serves us better to know that that's true.

Embracing Your Ideal Self Is One of the Arts of Happiness

It is human nature to become jealous of others and want to drag them down or speak ill of them. But if we can hold ourselves back and acknowledge others' outstanding attributes, abilities, efforts, and great achievements, it means that we have overcome our own barriers and grown. It also means that we have developed an eye for seeing other people's excellence and virtues and have become bighearted. People work hard and sometimes risk their lives for a person who recognizes their abilities. Recognition is powerful. We all seek recognition, but it's not an easy thing to earn. Nonetheless, we should know that other people seek it, just as we do. So instead of flatly denying others' abilities based on your subjective view, you need to realize the significance of cultivating a mindset of recognizing others' strengths.

It's worthwhile to practice seeing others from an objective perspective—with the eyes of a fellow human who was born in the same age or from the perspective of school, work, or society as a whole. When you do that, you're likely to notice their good aspects, for example diligence. Then you can simply recognize those qualities without getting jealous.

Cultivating this ability will bring growth to you as well as the other person. This is actually a wonderful ability to develop. When you recognize other people's positive qualities and attributes, you will grow. To be honest, I didn't quite understand this when I was young.

Conversely, those who think it's okay to speak ill of others are basically thinking that they don't have to make an effort to improve themselves any further. When you see someone receiving praise for getting a good score on a test, there are many ways you can talk about the person. For example, you can flatly deny the person's abilities and say, "He is actually very stupid and no good." Or you can diminish his abilities by saying, "It was only a fluke. It was blind luck," "He made no effort. His parents are smart, that's all," or "He was the teacher's pet." But when you recognize him and congratulate him by saying, "That's great!" your affirmation will become a driving force that pulls you up, as well as him. Embracing your ideal image means acknowledging the direction you're aiming for and bringing change to yourself.

When you recognize other people's strengths as your ideal, they'll open up to you and give you advice and guidance. This is how the human mind works, and I recommend that you all become aware of this principle. Young people especially have trouble overcoming their feelings of jealousy and accepting their strengths, so they should at least become aware of this principle as one of the arts for achieving happiness.

When You Compliment Others, Say What You Believe to Be True

Of course, there are wrong ways of complimenting others. It's wrong to praise others to take advantage of them, and it's wrong to make superficial remarks to flatter them. These kinds of compliments could be fine for someone you see very rarely or will never meet again, but if you say things that you don't believe to be true to people with whom you may form long-lasting relationships, they'll eventually find out that you were lying, making irresponsible remarks, or saying haphazard and dishonest things. They will feel betrayed and lied to and will no longer believe what you say. This would inflict great damage on your friendship.

So when you offer someone praise, it's a good idea to check whether you're telling the truth or expressing your true feelings. At any rate, it's not a good idea to compliment people with an intention of lying to them or deceiving them. It may be difficult to praise everything about a person, but you can still find and compliment some aspects of the person that you find genuinely praiseworthy.

To illustrate this, let's say there are two women who both want to get married, and one is stunningly good-looking and the other not as good-looking. It's not necessarily true that the better-looking woman will get married first. If the not-as-good-looking woman marries first, will the better-looking woman be able to give her blessings? It would be human nature to want to ask why the other woman was able to get married first. But that would make her just an ordinary person.

A person who is truly beautiful both inside and outside would be confident that she will eventually find someone perfect for her. If she feels this way and feels at ease, she'll be happy to see someone else get married, even if that person is less physically attractive than her. She can sincerely congratulate the bride, saying, "That's great! I'm really happy for you." In this way, she can not only continue the friendship, but also make her beauty shine even more. If a beautiful woman has a good nature, she'll be regarded even more highly. But a woman with a bitter heart is disliked, no matter how physically attractive she may be.

Women who have a keen interest in getting married may not be very happy when they go to other people's weddings. But they can make an effort to set aside their personal desires and look at the situation objectively, thinking, "She is really fortunate and perhaps lucky to be able to get married. It's great that someone I know is getting married." That will help them compliment the bride without having unpleasant feelings.

These compliments benefit not only the person whose life is blessed but also the person who gives the compliments. Other people will notice that the person who gives the compliment is a wonderful person and will want to bring happiness to such a person.

It's the same with studying. Naturally, some get good results while others don't, and there are times when you do well on tests and times when you don't. Yet, it would not be good to bash someone whose grades have improved or to belittle someone whose grades have gotten worse by saying, "Serves you right!"

Even if someone is smart and does well in his studies, if he speaks ill of others who get better results than his or treats someone whose results are poorer than his with contempt, no one will want him to become a leader. Those who honestly admire a person who gets good results and say, "You did well. That's great. How did you study?" are generous and wonderful people.

On the contrary, it's not good behavior to say things like "That's what you get!" or "I feel better!" to someone whose results are poor, nor is it a good thing for the person who says these things, though he may have been honest and felt relieved.

Whether you can have a heart that blesses others is one test of enlightenment to determine whether you'll be able to improve yourself. So please make an effort to cultivate a heart that blesses others.

3

The Heart of Blessing Lets Us Remedy Family Discord

Blessing Each Other Helps Heal Marital Discord

It can be hard to find a heart to bless others, but striving to do so from time to time can, at the very least, salve the poison of the various troubles and discord in our relationships.

We can all practice blessing others, including in our relationships with our spouses. During the year leading up to a divorce, there is a great deal of bickering. People may wonder why the two people in the marital conflict chose to marry someone they hated so much. Some couples that used to shower each other with praise and compliments when they were still in their dating stage or in the beginning years of their married lives may now find every discussion between them turning into an argument. The change in their relationship is so great. By looking at our partner through objective eyes, though, we can realize that not many people in this world deserve to be spoken only badly of.

Married couples must have fallen in love with each other at one point or another, and even if they were not exactly madly in love, some inner feeling must have said to them that their spouse would not be a bad choice for them. But now, one or another aspect of their partners bothers them, or they can no longer handle their partners' spiteful words, and their relationship starts to show signs of strain.

Then, as they exchange words of spite on a daily basis, they become convinced that the things that they say to each other are the truth. In the same way that newspaper editorials begin to sound like the truth when you casually read them, day in and day out, divorced couples begin to believe in the things they've said to each other and stop genuinely communicating.

When they first decided to get married, they surely didn't think of each other as such bad people. Perhaps there are some exceptional cases where one partner may find out that their other half is an incredibly horrid person only after they've tied the knot—but I think that cases like these happen very rarely. In most cases of marital conflict, the issue is how the partners see each other, because the partners have always been the same people that they were before. Even if something about them has changed, they are still largely the same person. What has truly changed is the perceptions they now hold of each other—their own personal views of each other.

So if you find yourself speaking badly of your spouse all the time, take one moment to stop yourself and look at your spouse objectively, from the viewpoint of the rest of society, and determine from this perspective whether your words are truly fair.

Valid Criticism Is Sometimes Necessary, But Ill Words Are Best Avoided

Words of spite and words of criticism can be similar, and sometimes it's hard to tell them apart. The person you're criticizing or throwing spiteful words at may not notice the difference between them. And sometimes this person is right: your criticisms aren't always valid.

But sometimes criticism is valid, and this is where criticism and words of spite may differ. To determine whether a criticism is valid, we can look at whether the thoughts behind it are sensible. Is there a good reason why the person we're criticizing should trust our words? Or do our criticisms arise from our own impulsive feelings?

I don't think we can make every criticism disappear; some criticism is a necessary part of our lives. But we don't want to continue speaking badly of others constantly if this has been our habit. If it is our habit, then we want to self-reflect and try to make amends. Sometimes, offering constructive criticism is a necessary part of helping people improve when something they're doing is not right, but being habitually critical is something that we want to mindfully self-examine. Thoroughly examine the reason for your criticism by asking yourself whether it's grounded in valid reasons or whether the actual source of your criticism is your own bad mood, feeling physically unwell, or feeling bothered about something.

With that said, if you want to avoid divorce, my advice for you is to offer your partner praise. Your praise shouldn't be based on falsehoods; doing that would only reflect back on you. But offer compliments based on aspects of him or her that you think are truly admirable. There is definitely some commendable aspect of your partner that can be praised. If you can't find it in yourself to compliment your partner's whole being, look for one or another aspect of your partner to praise, such as her good qualities or something she has been working hard to improve. This kind of praise will bring change to your partner's feelings and melt her frozen heart. By practicing giving each other praise in this way, both you and your partner will be able to come together and meet each other halfway.

In offering your partner praise, you allow her to realize that you're a nice person at heart, and this causes changes in her to occur, too. Your partner is actually a reflection of yourself in a mirror. When you throw ill words at him, you will be met with ill words thrown back at you. And when your heart blesses her, her heart will bless you, too. So it serves you best to make the effort to offer your partner compliments and praise.

What I have discussed so far is my advice for people in general. I should add to this, though, a word regarding cases in which one partner's role in society advances very considerably, widening the chasm between each partner's sense of responsibility to society. One partner may not be able to understand why the other is prioritizing professional responsibilities so much, and this may make him or her want to criticize one-sidedly. If the gap between the two partners' values becomes too wide in this way, in some cases both will be happier in the end if they decide to part ways.

Fairness toward Well-Behaved and Misbehaving Children Is Precious Parenting Practice

Children can also have a habit of speaking badly of others. Some children who speak ill of others need their parents to give them guidance and stern rebukes so they will change this habit. But there is a common pitfall that parents often walk into in these cases.

When you're raising more than one child, it's natural to find variations between your children in their personal growth and sense of right and wrong. Parents who are of a socialist frame of mind sometimes want to protect the ill-behaved child in an effort to make up for this gap that they find between their children, and this wish to treat everyone equally may lead them to go further by criticizing their children who are behaving well and refraining from offering them praise. This is something that I hope that parents will take care not to do.

It's important to love your children equally, but this love has more to do with a basic, fundamental truth. It has to do with everyone's equality as children of God, the equality of everyone's divine nature, or the right to happiness that each person in this world received equally from God.

There are differences, however, in each individual child's actions, deeds, effort, daily life, and words, which can be right or wrong or deserving or not deserving of praise, and which may, if parents lump all these things equally together, negatively impact the adults that their children grow up to be. To improve your ability to educate your children, you need to be capable of distinguishing between these things.

Trying too hard to treat each of your children equally and blaming society for their faults may lead them to make mistakes as adults. This may lead them to think that it is society, not themselves, that's in the wrong.

So as parents, you need to treat each of your children according to your honest assessment of their behavior rather than sugarcoating your words or rebuking them. Avoid overdoing your effort to treat all of them equally. Your children need you to observe their behavior and educate them to value one behavior over others. If one of your children shows bad behavior or an ill attitude toward daily life, you should make as much of an effort as possible to teach and guide that child to understand which behaviors and attitudes are desirable and which are unwanted, through the culture and atmosphere you create in your household.

As I touched on earlier, by treating wayward children with too much leniency and refraining from giving your upright children well-deserved praise, you'll let the wayward children continue to misbehave and disobey you even in their adulthood. This is an issue about their habits. As adults, they will continue to rely on you financially, burden you with troubles, and require you to look after them. In contrast, it's the good or upright children who usually come to look after you in the end. But throughout the time that these children are supporting you in your old age, they'll carry with them a very deep sense of frustration about the biased and unfair treatment they received during childhood. Even though they'll be at your side, they'll still achingly remember the praise and protection you gave the wayward children and the little recognition that they, the good children, received for their deeds. So I think that it's important for all parents to know that it's undesirable and wrong for parents to continue judging their children based on unfair reasons.

Earning Parents' Trust Should Be a Basic Goal of Our Childhood

Several hundred years ago in Japan, someone once wrote about an effective way to distinguish whether or not your child is a good son or daughter. This person wrote: Your child is a good son or daughter to you if, when you hear that news has been going around about your child, you think of him or her receiving praise. In contrast, your child is a wayward son or daughter if hearing about this brings up images in your mind of your child getting into trouble or the spread of bad rumors concerning your child. I think that these are reflection points that give us a reliable yardstick.

During your twenties and thirties, if you would like to consider whether you have grown up to be a good son or daughter, consider the thoughts that will go through your parents' minds when they hear that there's been news floating around about you. Do you imagine them worrying whether you might have gotten into trouble again? Or do you see them trusting you and assuming that whatever the rumor is, it concerns a praiseworthy accomplishment?

Another point to consider is what would happen if you told your parents that you're considering going abroad. They may not want to give you their consent if they fear that you'll continue to create trouble abroad, because they know how much mischief you have caused at home. You may wish to retaliate and want to believe that your parents are out to suppress your independence. But their reaction is just the result of the lack of trust that you've built with them over the course of your childhood. Your parents wouldn't disagree with your idea if they trusted your ability to live abroad on your own and overcome any difficulties you might face. But if you can imagine yourself receiving your parents' consent, that shows that you earned their trust during your childhood years. I think that this shows how good a son or daughter you must have been to them.

So the first, basic step is to gain your parents' trust,

which will gradually lead to gaining the trust of your friends and your superiors and associates at work. It will serve your life in the long run to begin by striving to gain your parents' trust during your childhood. When your parents hear that there's been word going around concerning you, will they brace themselves for ill news or will they expect glad tidings? The answer to this question often indicates the difference between the good and bad children. And if your parents did receive ill news about you, would they believe it? Or would they disbelieve it and wonder whether it might be due to some type of misunderstanding? If they would disbelieve ill news about you, that's another sign that you've been a good child to them and evidence of the trust you've built with them on a daily basis.

Parents of children with the right daily attitude toward life have no qualms about seeing them leave home and go out into the world. Children who have caused their parents a lot of worry throughout childhood, however, will continue to fill their parents with concern when they go out into the real world. Considering these points will give you a good sense of whether you've been a good child or not.

If, right now, you are already past the age of thirty-five and aren't sure whether you've been a good child to your parents, these same things are good points to reflect on. If your parents were to receive a phone call about you, would their hearts begin to race? Your answer to this question will give you a basic idea of what kind of child you've been to them.

Trust is built by accumulating small amounts of effort over the course of many years. Trust isn't instantly earned out of thin air, but neither can it be easily wiped out in a single blow. An impactful event or doing of a considerable degree needs to occur for trust to be earned or lost. A certain degree of effort is required to earn a favorable judgment instead of a bad one and to gain others' trust, and making efforts is clearly the direction we need to focus on.

4

Practising Blessing Others to Solve Our Workbook of Life

Prayer and Fighting Fiercely are Both Necessary Practices in Opposing Clear Evil

As this chapter has emphasized, ill words, jealous emotions, and dwelling on others' faults are acts that don't lead to happiness. Instead, we need to practice the heart that blesses others.

But then, you may wonder what you should do when you encounter true evil. When someone has committed an evil act, you may want to know whether you should give that person your blessing. If one of your acquaintances is a serial killer, for example, is that someone you should also pay compliments to?

I think it's impossible to support and praise a person who has committed an act of pure evil. Doing so would naturally be an act of falsehood and dishonesty. Instead, please offer your prayers for this person. Pray to heaven for this person to turn over a new leaf, find the path to good deeds, stop committing evil acts, and find salvation of the soul. And if you can think of anything else that may help this person, please do that as well.

Sometimes, the evil you encounter holds a clear, strong intention, and you'll need to fight against that intention. Happy Science has also practiced such things many times in the past. We at Happy Science often practice an open mind and a heart of acceptance. We always wish to give praise to things that deserve praise. But we also don't hesitate to fight mightily against clear evil when such things need to be hindered from further growth. It was the same in Buddhism, when the historical Buddha fought fiercely against the Devil and people's evil acts. We're aware that this can affect us negatively and cause us suffering, but we don't let that stop us from fighting evil when it's necessary. Denying ourselves the option to fight evil might allow the evil to grow and spread. Should you ever find yourself in this situation, consider the good or evil or righteous or unrighteous nature of what you're faced with in as thorough a manner as possible, and then make your decision.

When looking at each individual person, however, we need to understand that we human beings make mistakes, so a certain amount of tolerance and acceptance is necessary. We want to find the positive points in people, guide them in the right direction, and help them change themselves one step at a time.

The Heart that Blesses Those You Envy Will Save You from Jealous Feelings

It's often said that the opposite of love is hatred, but some say that love's real opposite is jealousy. This may well be true. Jealous thoughts bring us suffering and sleepless nights. But a heart that blesses others will save us from this suffering.

If blessing others is not something you can find it in yourself to do yet, then you can think about your words of blessing within your heart or out loud when you're all by yourself. You'll feel much better, and the energy from your thoughts of blessing will surely be felt by the people you're sending them to.

Earlier in this chapter, I spoke about issues that parents are faced with when assessing their wayward and upright children and also about the need to hinder people from committing evil deeds. To these topics, I should add that there are situations at work in which one's competency at one's job needs to be seriously considered. You may need to look into mistakes your employees make but also give recognition to those who are succeeding. Twisting the facts and evaluating people unfairly is the wrong thing to do.

At the same time, we also need to practice the saying, "Hate the sin, not the sinner." You can offer criticism and deny the job and results of someone's work, but you also need a heart to embrace the deeper aspects of the person's human nature. That is, your criticisms should pertain to just the person's work.

You should also cherish the innate talents of those you feel jealous of. If someone has demonstrated talent and achieved excellent results, she may be someone who is loved by God or has accumulated these abilities over the course of many past lives. So, you should bless these aspects of her.

You may think that it's strange for someone else to be succeeding even though you're working harder than he is, but a reason may exist for this that's not limited to this present life. The reason may also be found in things you're not aware of that have to do with what you've accumulated in your past lives. This is how we should think in such circumstances.

Having a heart of blessing is also a type of enlightenment. I hope that what I've discussed in this chapter will give you hints about how to solve the problems in your unique workbook of life.

CHAPTER FOUR

living through the giant waves of adversity

1

Relying On Faith to Guide You through Adversity

Life's Worries Can Be Solved

In this chapter, I would like to talk about living through the giant waves of destiny's hardships. This image may give you the sense that life is a fateful journey with ups and downs, and we are much like fish making their way through the battering whirlpools of the sea.

But I would like you to know that, when the highs and lows of life eventually pass, they will all transform into wonderful memories. Of course, adversities can appear unrelenting when we're in the midst of them. Hindsight may let us see that these hardships had been trifling issues, but they seem like a huge ordeal in our lives when we're in the throes of them.

Like everyone else, I used to anguish over the troubles and hardships that faced me. But the final outcome or result of each one revealed to me that they had not been worth the fuss, in spite of my misery. This is what happens to us when in the throes of a difficulty, no matter who we may be. People around us can tell when our issues are trifling and typical. But we, who are standing in the midst of them, can only picture them as terrible waves of adversity tossing us about mercilessly.

What I would like to talk about is how we can learn to see current adversities as small hardships and bring peace and tranquility to the heaving waves of our mind. This is an important part of our spiritual discipline.

Let Your Faith Point You in the Right Direction

Problems are a part of the lives of everyone. I think that no one has ever managed to go through life problem-free. If a problem is troubling you right now, this is a proof that you are alive and living in this very moment. In a sense, finding that all of your problems have disappeared is kind of like a sign telling you that it's your time to depart from this world.

Furthermore, your worry over your problems is a sign that you may be able to solve them by looking at them differently. In some sense, the problems you face are a "test from the gods" to help you discover how much adversity you can endure.

My spiritual awakening came to me when I was twenty-four years old. But, looking back, my twenties were a time when I was confronted with day-to-day issues that were difficult to fully resolve. I remember this period as a time when every problem I resolved was always followed by yet another one. Even after I resigned from the company I was working for and started this religion, troubles concerning how to run the organization kept emerging one after another. Once I overcame one wave, it was as if the next wave had been waiting to engulf me. When I overcame that one, there was yet another wave that came quickly rushing in.

In such times in life, the most important thing to do is not lose our sense of direction: we need to remember which way leads to the open sea and which way points to the safety of the shore. Giant waves will inevitably come, and when they do, we won't be able to save ourselves if we swim in the direction of the sea. But if we know at least to swim toward the shore, we'll surely find a way to escape at some point. This is a decision between two choices, and it's a decision we can't afford to get wrong.

So is there some way to determine whether we're headed in the direction of the shore or the open sea in the midst of adversity? If you're a Happy Science believer, it's good to take the standpoint of faith to decide whether a certain direction is the right one. Your faith should be the basis of your decision. If your faith tells you that the direction is right, then it is paramount to swim in that direction without hesitation, even in the face of a big wave approaching from that direction. Conversely, a direction that you feel is against your faith will be the wrong one to take, and you'll need to turn around and change course. Despite its simplicity, this is a point that you want to keep in your heart, for the course of your life may otherwise fall to the mercy of adversities, and you mustn't let this happen.

Check for the Tendency to Love Unhappiness

Some people seem to find delight in the waves of troubles they face and swim toward them, even to the point of feeling as if they're drowning and gasping for air. If this has been the case with you, you will need to resolve this pattern of mind. In several of my books, including *The Unhappiness Syndrome**, I've mentioned that we humans seldom notice our tendency to love unhappiness, and I think that this mindset exists in everyone. While others may easily be able to point out this aspect of you, it can be a difficult thing to recognize by yourself.

Past events that brought you sadness, suffering, and failure may have become engraved into your heart and led you to develop a failure-based mindset. When a similar situation crops up to remind you of your past experiences, the failure-seeking pattern steers you in the direction of further failure, so you may find yourself repeating your experiences over and over, whether at work or in human relationships. The hint of a past setback makes you brace yourself in anticipation, which itself invites the very same events to occur again.

We humans tend to blame our external circumstances and the people around us for the misfortunes in our lives. We seldom realize that there is a failure-seeking pattern of our own making that is leading

---

* Ryuho Okawa, *The Unhappiness Syndrome* (New York: IRH Press, 2017).

us to repeat our unhappy experiences. This is the reason that those who are unhappy bring further unhappiness upon themselves.

If similar misfortunes have struck you twice, three times, or more, take a step back and take a third-party perspective to observe yourself. Take a middle-way perspective to look within yourself with a clean mental slate.

Put an End to the Yearning for Sympathy

I often teach that the practice of giving love to others is important. But in the end, we humans cannot do otherwise but seek to be loved. Being loved by another is a delight indeed and gives us happiness, so we seek others' love.

But sometimes we don't receive the love that we wish for, and in compensation, sometimes we begin behaving in ways designed to draw others' sympathy. We deliberately put ourselves in a position that is sure to invite other people's compassion.

You can imagine to a certain extent what kinds of situations will draw people's sympathy. For example, getting ill is one such situation. A hostile enemy or a rival may change their attitude toward you the minute you become sick, end their attacks, and start to show you kindness. There are some people who, when they don't have enough courage to offer to make up, escape the conflict by becoming sick instead of making an effort to reconcile.

Also, a love of poverty is something that an unexpectedly large number of people share. Many such people often place the blame for their failures or impoverished circumstances on the people around them, their company, their country, and the world economy. This group of people includes not just the average worker, but also corporate CEOs.

If you have the tendency to seek sympathy from others, it will better serve you to put an end to this inclination. Gathering sympathy will seldom improve your situation in the true sense. The words of comfort you receive will not lead to a true solution to your problem.

2

The Mindset that Determines Your Happiness or Unhappiness in Life

Seek Not Equal Outcomes, But Equal Opportunities for Everyone

The phrase "the working poor," has become popular in my country of Japan and has given me much reason for concern. This phrase refers to the impoverished but working class of people whose lives have seen little improvement despite the efforts they've always been putting into their work. On television and in newspapers, this topic has received wide coverage, including in featured television programs and media articles.

This way of understanding the condition of today's working poor sounds to me to be a kind of communist thinking. This is the type of thinking that, when it is followed, leads to blaming the government, the world, and the small number of smart, wealthy people for the poor people's suffering, which is the same basic idea underlying the philosophy of communism. In essence, communism is a philosophy that rationalizes jealousy. It is basically a justification of jealousy toward successful people.

Succeeding in a communist society leads to being the target of many people's jealousy, so the aim of such a society becomes avoiding individual success and realizing equality of outcomes among everyone. This striving for common equality, however, leads to the impoverishment of society as a whole. To some, this may sound like the right idea to follow, because then everyone will share in the suffering of poverty. But no one with the power to help the poor will remain. This is an often-occurring plight of societies established on communist principles.

So as we pursue equality, my earnest recommendation is to adopt the following way of thinking. The equality we should seek, that I strive to promote, is equality of opportunity, or equal chances to all people. I believe that everyone should have at least a chance to succeed, and we want to make as many such opportunities available as possible.

But you cannot expect equal results. Just as the runners of a 100-meter competition or a 26.2-mile (42 km) marathon will cross the finish lines at varying times and their performances will differ from person to person, all runners may deserve praise for their efforts, but there will always be individual variations in scores and placements.

The same holds true in academic and artistic achievements. If the artistic genius and the amateur artist were to receive the same level of recognition from others, what do you think would be the result? Everyone would probably stop striving to make an effort, because creating exceptional works of art would cease to hold value. If society gave equal recognition to a masterpiece of a lifetime and an average piece of artwork, then no one would feel the need to create outstanding works of art any more.

In reality, an outstanding, award-winning painting such as those we find at the Japan Fine Arts Exhibition will receive an appraisal based on a price per unit of measurement, and may be valued at anywhere from hundreds of thousands to millions of dollars. The dream to achieve this recognition has been the motivation for budding painters who have put their hearts and souls into their work.

The same holds true for musicians, who would all cease to strive to give their best performances if all of them were to be rewarded equally. Or imagine what would happen to the world of professional baseball if the salaries of star players of the likes of Hideki Matsui and Ichiro were decreased to match those of other players who don't perform as well, because we all believe in the principle of equality. I think that even Matsui and Ichiro would gradually find their motivation waning and would probably stop putting in effort, leading them to perform poorly.

Seeking Sympathy Doesn't Win You Supporters in the End

The *chance* of success should be guaranteed to everyone, but there will have to be differences in outcomes, which are the results of each individual's effort, perseverance, and innate talent and the support and encouragement that each of us receives from others.

It's been said by someone who isn't affiliated with a religious organization that for most types of endeavor we pursue, we have a chance of succeeding if we gain the support of three hundred people. Of course, the successful development of a religious organization requires the support of a tremendous number of people, but even in this case, I think that the support of three hundred people will still allow you to establish a small one. Currently, more than 180,000 religious organizations exist in Japan alone, and my country probably has approximately three hundred believers per religious organization.

The backing of this many people's assistance can help any kind of undertaking take flight. You are certain to succeed in any career you choose, whether as a singer, a restaurant or beauty salon owner, or in any other type of occupation of any industry. Your ability to gather the appreciation and support of many people is extremely important.

Many people who are focused on trying to gain other people's sympathy overlook this aspect of success. Three hundred people will not want to offer you their backing if you're seeking to find relief from your miserable circumstances. Perhaps they'll show you kindness at first, but they'll gradually grow weary of your claims on them after the second or third time you come to them looking for sympathy.

In today's aging society, we have increasing numbers of elderly people, many of whom probably have a lot of pent up frustration toward their children, children-in-law, and grandchildren, and those who are kind will lend their ears to these elders' words. As I've said, though, they may listen to their elders' frustrations in the beginning, but they may grow tired of them by the second or third visit. After the fourth time, they may stop visiting, and then there will be no one to talk to, as often occurs.

Happiness, in large part, is hard to attain by seeking sympathy. The type of person who brings happiness to others, not the type of person who seeks to receive others' kindness, is the kind of person whom others wish to visit repeatedly. The type of person who influences you positively or inspires you with each visit, who offers hints that benefit your life, who is your source of courage, who is a shoulder to lean on when you're feeling down and in need of encouragement—this is the person whom people want to come to see, many times over, over the course of years.

What we need to do is to turn around our way of thinking. The more sensitive our disposition is, the more inclined we are to seek kindness, and if you've taken on such a tendency, making an effort to change your way of thinking will be essential to you.

Make Other People, Not Yourself, the Center of Focus

Let me explain what I've discussed so far from another angle. The concepts of geocentrism and heliocentrism give us alternative theories about the positioning of the sun and the earth. Heliocentrism is the theory that the earth revolves around the sun as the center, and geocentrism is the theory that the sun revolves around the earth as the center. If we judge based on our everyday physical senses, we may think that geocentrism is the truth, but the real truth is that the earth is revolving at a tremendous speed around the sun. As far as our physical senses go we on earth feel as if we are the ones who are stationary and the sun must be revolving around us and the earth. This is what people of ancient times believed to be the truth.

Like this misunderstanding, there are some of us who believe that the world revolves around ourselves as the fixed center, an illusion that's formed as we live through each of the days of our lives. Perhaps there are some people whose lives at home revolve around their father or husband, and others that revolve around the mother or wife. People who are treated like they're the center of things may tend to think that everyone functions around them or that everyone else is supposed to accommodate their interests. So we can say that some people live with geocentric mindsets and others live with heliocentric mindsets.

Our planet, Earth, is not only revolving around the sun, but is also constantly rotating on its own axis, but this fact is difficult to realize while we are carrying out our daily lives on its surface. But by looking at time-lapse photos of the evening skies, we can see that the stars are moving across the skies every day.

When I went to Hawaii to give a lecture there some time ago, I dined at a scenic restaurant where I somehow saw the stars moving steadily on their paths in the evening sky. Looking up at them, it was hard to imagine that the ground lying beneath me was truly moving, not the skies and stars that looked to be the ones traveling. The cause of the unhappiness we all experience can be found in this same kind of misperception. This geocentric misperception is the mindset we want to correct when we're facing difficulties and hardships.

The advice I am offering in this chapter is simple. What it boils down to is that we need to change our geocentric perceptions, our self-centered mindsets, and doing so will improve our human relationships and help us fundamentally improve our work. Saying to ourselves, "I need to be the one to take action" is the heliocentric perspective, which is the mindset of always thinking about how we can better serve our customers.

In contrast, the geocentric mindset in a work environment is like thinking, "I don't see what's wrong with our products. It's the customers' fault for not wanting to buy them." Or it makes you blame the supermarket or department store for putting your mom-and-pop store out of business, leading you to participate in demonstrations against expanding supermarkets and department stores.

When we think with a customer-based mindset, we see that customers benefit from better services overall if the businesses that offer superior services survive the market. Large supermarket franchises have their own benefits. Since they're able to stock products and goods in large volumes, they are capable of offering their customers a larger variety of products at lower price points. For small shops to survive in this market, then, they need to provide services that large supermarkets and department stores are unable to offer, such as custom-order deliveries directly to customers' homes and a selection of products that can't be found on large supermarket shelves. Practicing this kind of a mental attitude of striving to fulfill your customers' needs is essential.

We can basically think of ourselves as either having a heliocentric or geocentric pattern of mind. Which of these two patterns your own mental attitude leans toward can determine the happiness or unhappiness and the success or lack of success of your life. We naturally have feelings of dislike toward people who are self-centered, but it's difficult to realize it when we ourselves have fallen into a self-centered mindset. We feel unpleasant around people who are egocentric, because we can tell that they're thinking only about themselves and are going through their lives as their own ego pleases them. It's very easy to recognize and criticize such people. But we become oblivious to this mindset when it comes to realizing this about ourselves. This is the reason why, through my teaching on self-reflection, I teach people to reflect on themselves as if they were looking at their reflection in a mirror, and through my teaching of love, I teach people to treat others as they would wish others to treat them.

3

Decisiveness Will Open a Path for You

You Need to Make a Decision in the End

For people like business executives who bear the burden of large responsibilities, some of the waves of destiny's hardships may be especially large and often bring very tough times. They may feel as if wave after wave of large problems that need to be solved are swallowing them up. In the midst of such times, what's important is for these executives to make decisions based on their faith. The second point of vital importance I would like to raise is about decisiveness itself. The ability to make decisions is a crucial aspect of our lives.

When people have become trapped in a spiral of despair or find themselves bobbing in and out of the waves, gasping for breath, they are typically suffering from indecision. Being able to make a decision is of great significance in such times. When indecision plagues us, our heads continue to rise out of the water only to sink again. What I mean to say by this analogy is that our minds keep swaying back and forth without a set direction.

This physical world we live in consists of clashing values. A variety of values exist among individuals as well as organizations, and it's not that all of them are wrong—there are good aspects to each of them—which is what leads to clashing values. Yet what we need to do in the final analysis is make our own decision. The possible ways and methods of operating a business are countless but, in the end, we need to make a decision. A final decision has to be made. It's so important to our lives that we train ourselves to have courage in making decisions and strive to become more decisive.

A Story about My Decision to Start Happy Science

In the mid-1980s, I spent one or two years working in the Nagoya office of the company I was working for. I had already begun preparing myself to eventually resign from this company, and it was about a month after I was transferred back to their office in Tokyo that I resigned to start my religious organization, Happy Science. If I hadn't made that decision at that time, Happy Science may not be what it is now.

When this company first hired me, I only saw it as a result of total chance, but over time, I saw how interesting my job was becoming to me, and my job became a joy. It's part of the nature of jobs that they become more interesting as we put more work into them. I was eventually entrusted to handle jobs of greater importance, and those around me began to count on me more frequently. So it was very difficult to decide to leave the company at this time. This company was a general trading company that ranked seventh globally and reported thirty billion dollars of annual sales, which at the time was comparable to the annual sales of the Toyota Motor Corporation.

Toward the end of the period that I worked for this company, I was in the accounting and finances department of the Nagoya office and in charge of dealing with the banks. Because of the high-volume purchasing and sales that trading companies do, large funds are a necessity. So in preparation for times that required all the funds that we could possibly gather, we were constantly borrowing slightly more money from the bank than was actually necessary.

Moreover, this was during the 1980s in the midst of a bubble economy in Japan, a time when the bank was telling my company that property values would only keep increasing over time and that any land we purchased with borrowed money would eventually pay for itself. My company took this advice, borrowed more than it actually needed, and put the extra funds into extraneous business such as purchasing land and developing golf courses, bowling alleys, and apartment complexes. The company was bringing in thirty billion dollars in sales but borrowing over ten billion dollars from the bank, if I remember correctly. It was more than clear to me that this company was overborrowing. I reached the conclusion that this plan of limitless borrowing posed great risk to the company, that any further extraneous borrowing would need to be curbed, and that the company needed to realize that it was holding an excessive amount of debt in long-term loans.

To be more precise, the trading company was being forced to borrow from the bank because of the great influence that banks held at the time. Trading companies were some of the banks' largest clients and could contract loans of as much as one billion dollars. The banks much preferred to issue large, long-term loans that gave them higher profits than small, short-term loans, which were tiresome and gave them small returns.

What I found most problematic at this company was its large amount of debt in long-term loans with fixed interest at nearly 10 percent, which I think the company had been pushed into agreeing with. The banks had higher status than the trading company and would send their most elite and proud representatives to coerce the company into taking out these loans. They were very tough people to deal with. This was a time when long-term lenders such as the Industrial Bank of Japan and the Long-Term Credit Bank of Japan employed large numbers of high and mighty University of Tokyo graduates.

It was the task of negotiating with these people that my trading company often assigned to me, as the company's so-called "destroyer of elites"—its special trump card. Perhaps they saw me as what would have long ago been a kind of seasoned, fearless samurai assassin with an attitude of never hesitating to resort to street assassination. I was called in to deal with these difficult representatives whenever they came from the banks. I was an unrelenting negotiator. I always defeated my opponents and brought home the trophy to my company, and this must have made me a very convenient person for the company.

I Knew that My Decision Would Allow Me to Spread More Happiness

Shortly before I left the company, there was a company-wide invitation to submit an essay, so I wrote one to propose my ideas about the direction I thought the company should head. During the evaluation process, my essay went all the way up to the directors and nearly reached the company president. But because my essay included a clear critique of the president's management policies and a warning against the risks they posed, his advisors chose not to give me an award, which would have meant that everyone in the company would have read my essay. So, after some behind-the-scenes discussions, they decided not to show my essay to the president, and this is how it became a phantom essay.

Once I left the trading company, though, it did make policy shifts based on the scenario I had written about in my essay. The company managed to hold together for a time, but in the early 2000s it faced a management crisis due to mistakes in cash management and financial planning, and it merged with another trading company to avoid going under. According to people who knew me, this outcome would've been avoided if I had not left. My friends may have had a point. With the kind of foresight I possessed, I would probably have been able to prevent the same mistakes from being made, which would have allowed the company to survive their crisis.

I was aware that many people in the company had been pinning their hopes on me, trusting me, and investing greatly in me as one of their best, which made my decision to leave a difficult one. But I had spent the previous year preparing to create my religious organization. And I knew that after I left, I would have no job nor any income at all to support myself. Making this decision caused me much heartache while I was working in Nagoya. And virtually all my suffering of that last year or so with them came down to the difficulty of this decision in front of me. The spiritual message series was already being written during this time, but I faced a lot of anguish because I lacked enough inner conviction from not having enough know-how about establishing and developing a religious organization. Also, I was gradually being entrusted to handle the company's more important tasks, and it brought me so much pain to know that, despite the hopes that were being set upon me, I was going to be leaving and letting them down.

After I left, I saw that the company restructured. A considerable number of employees were laid off and, as I said earlier, the company ultimately had to accept a merger. Even so, I had the sense back then that creating Happy Science and spreading the Truths throughout Japan and the world would bring happiness to a greater number of people, and this would allow me to more than make up for the disadvantages I'd bring to the company by leaving. Even though I felt deep remorse, I knew I had to be decisive, and I saw that there was no other possible choice.

Because I had already spotted the flaws in the president's policy, I can confidently say that my staying with them would have helped prevent the company's ruin. I knew that my leaving couldn't be helped, however. The world is, indeed, undergoing constant change—all things are impermanent. In the face of market competition, it's only natural that some businesses will inevitably face harsh events such as collapse.

I saw the company's history of eighty-something-years come to an end through their merger. I also saw the complete destruction of my former workplace inside the World Trade Center building in New York City by a hijacked passenger airplane. Events like these have shown me how many things in life can change very unexpectedly.

It is beyond human ability to know what kind of fate may awaits us. Whatever must come will come regardless, and no matter what it may be, we need to get through each new development with wisdom and decisiveness. Happy Science is working in earnest to become a world religion. We need to keep working until we reach this goal. Should we ever choose to give up, it will mean the end of this goal.

How Much You Let Go of Accords with How Much You Succeed in Life

To conclude, I would like to give you a summary of what I wanted to tell you in this chapter. There will be various times in the course of your life when giant waves of adversity will assail you, but please look to

---

* Ryuho Okawa, *Inochi No Ho* ["*The Laws of Life*"] (Tokyo: IRH Press, 2007).

your faith, and with this faith as your basis, assess which direction you think is the right one and resolve to go in that direction. Practicing decisiveness is crucial. There will be many times in life when letting go of something is a necessary part of moving forward. When you find yourself in such times, ponder carefully and decide to let go of the things that you know must be abandoned, even in spite of the pain this will bring you, and choose those things you must choose. As I have also written in another of my books, *The Laws of Life**, how much you are able to let go of accords with how much you succeed in life, as described by the law of compensation. Decisive moments are inevitably accompanied by pain, but it's important to know that this is a necessary part of opening the door to a new future for you and the world.

CHAPTER FIVE

feel the miracle

1

The True Cause of Our Suffering

The Desire to Protect Yourself Is Causing Your Unhappiness

In this chapter, I would like to focus on some essential points on the subject of miracles.

The practice of effort is at the very heart of the overall body of my teachings in Happy Science. But as with anything else, there is another side to this teaching.

Perhaps some of you reading this book have been making an effort, every day, to free yourself from inner anguish and suffering, but you have not been able to do so. If this has been the case with you, please ponder the reason for the anguish or pain you presently feel. You will most likely see that the cause of your inner pain comes down to this sole source: thoughts that desperately want to protect yourself. Can you see that the need to defend your feelings is causing you to think in a certain way? Please try to examine this point.

The need to defend ourselves from getting hurt was imbued into us physiologically, just as it was also given to insects and animals, and it's something we naturally act upon as human beings. But these decisions we make to follow our natural urges include an aspect that sadly leads to unhappiness. The desire to protect ourselves from getting hurt causes 90 percent of our suffering in life.

Justifying Our Unhappiness Is One Way We Try to Protect Ourselves

One shape that the need to defend ourselves takes is self-justification. Self-justification is when we search for excuses to validate our inner pain.

For example, perhaps you think that your suffering, inner anguish, or hurt feelings were caused by someone's words or actions, or perhaps there was an accident five years ago, you went through difficult times while having your child a decade ago, or you faced a setback the year you graduated from college, two decades ago. We often search outside ourselves—in the circumstances of our environment, the times we live in, or the conditions of our society—for the cause of our hurt feelings and pain. It can be the words and actions of others, external occurrences and events, the social conditions of the world, circumstances at work, or issues concerning our parents and children. We're bound to find one or another cause from among our surroundings to justify our inner pain. It's virtually impossible not to find any, and we can probably come up with at least two or three rationales for our suffering straightaway.

However, the natural urge to defend yourself may be at work, creating excuses to justify your unhappiness. And you are probably finding these in things outside yourself rather than within. You're probably thinking of the group of various events that have occurred in your life thus far and getting excuses from the words, actions, and feelings of the people around you. But one of the causes of your unhappiness is this mental attitude itself.

Your desire to defend yourself is supposed to stop you from getting hurt, but instead, it sometimes leads you to explain and validate your unhappiness to yourself. You tell yourself that you're unhappy because of other people; because of your weakened vision, poor hearing, or other physical ailments, because you're not smart enough, and various other reasons.

It's difficult to deny that this is true. You know that these feelings are there. You may not wish to readily acknowledge them, but they are certain to slip from your lips when you're by yourself. This strong desire to believe that your unhappiness is justified is, in fact, one of the main causes of your suffering.

Assailing Others Is Another Way We Try to Protect Ourselves

Another shape that the need to defend ourselves takes is the urge to assail others. This desire is often found in people with bullish, determined personalities. People like this don't just think passively and believe that they've fallen victim to outer circumstances. Instead, their thoughts say, "This person hurt me," or "This person is at fault for my failure." Such thoughts foster feelings of resentment, enmity, and rage, the desire for vengeance, a habit of relentless faultfinding, and the wish to ruin other people's lives. They may also lead to scheming behind the scenes and spreading ill rumors to bring the other person misery.

People of this type are everywhere, but they aren't necessarily evil people. In the end, their behavior is also motivated by the wish to protect themselves. People with one or another exceptional strength—a strong-willed mind, great vitality, assertiveness, or a high level of ability—tend to act on the offensive and aren't necessarily all evil people.

People with more passive personalities tend to use self-justification defensively. In contrast, people who are more self-assured tend to take the offensive. They accuse other people of wrongdoing, because that way someone else is the "villain" who takes the blame and they can excuse themselves for their own mistakes. They convince themselves that blaming someone else will resolve their own suffering. To resolve their suffering at work, for example, they'll blame the president of their company or, on a national scale, the president or prime minister of their country. If their child's grades are suffering, they'll blame the teacher for not being well educated enough, the school for having selected the wrong textbooks, or the cram school teacher for having inadequate teaching skills. Deep down inside, however, they realize that other children in the same school are achieving better results.

What I'm trying to say is that they are the type of people who criticize the school when they see their own child failing, while other people's children get accepted into junior high schools, high schools, or the universities of their choice. But if their own child succeeds, they shower the teacher with infinite praise. But as I've said, such people are not necessarily bad at heart. They're just the ordinary, typical people of our society who demonstrate a common state of mind shared by many people in general.

These types take the offensive, blaming their child's cram school or teacher for their own child's failure, all to defend themselves. Introverted types, on the other hand, place responsibility on their own family and blame their child's poor aptitude, their or their spouse's own lack of aptitude, the father's constant absence from home because of work, or lack of financial means.

So some people search inward to explain their unhappiness, while others search outward. But when we trace either of these back to their source, we arrive at the same thing: the need to defend ourselves.

Happy Science teaches the practice of self-reflection.

By using this teaching, you can carefully contemplate whether you have the desire to protect yourself, and I hope that you will put this into practice. You most likely have these feelings somewhere within you, and they are the real cause of the inner anguish and suffering you may be facing now.

2

Calmly Accept Your Workbook of Life

Sufferings Occur because They Are Meant To

I normally teach the practice of effort as the way to overcome worries and hardships. But since the theme of this chapter is experiencing miracles, I would like to discuss some things that may sound different from my usual self-help teachings.

As I've said, inner suffering arises from our desire to protect ourselves. But if we want to truly overcome our inner suffering, trying to make our sufferings go away won't help. Instead, please simply let go of trying.

Please let go of trying to blame yourself or others for your unhappiness. Let go of blaming your children. Look at everything that's unfolding in front of your eyes right now, and embrace all of it as a set of life events that are meant to be happening. These events aren't happening because of a mistake that you or someone else made solely by coincidence. The issues occupying your mind and making you suffer right now are meant to be happening to you, to send you the problems that you need to face in your life right now.

Let's look at times of illness as an example. People don't fall ill because they intended to. Illness comes to us, in fact, when we least expect it.

Illness can be caused by many things, including neglect of our physical health, lack of exercise, excessive stress, and poor nutritional balance. All these things help explain why we have gotten sick from the perspective of this physical world.

But there is another reason for times of illness. Illness ultimately occurs because it is a necessary experience for the age or standing in life that we've reached at that particular time in our lives.

Another type of suffering is failure. When we flunk an exam, for instance, it isn't the result of a stroke of bad luck; this problem is trying to show us a problem about ourselves that we need to work on solving at this point in our life. The lesson we need to learn may be that we haven't been putting in enough effort or that we need to realize the harsh reality of this world. Or perhaps flunking the exam is a way of thwarting us from a path that would lead to our future downfall or from an overgrown conceit, and maybe it's meant to remind us of the need for a persevering spirit. In any case, it is important for you to know that the phenomenon that is currently manifesting in your life is not a coincidence. The problem you're facing now is the appropriate one for your life at this particular time.

The same holds true if you're suffering from your child's ill behavior or a congenital physical disability. There is definitely a meaning behind these problems. There's meaning behind marital issues, as well. Conflicts with your spouse always have underlying reasons that have caused them, including the reasons why they're happening at this particular time in your life, and they're trying to teach you something important. As a matter of fact, marital problems arise at the essential time in your life to give you an important learning experience for your inner growth.

So, please grasp hold of the lessons within your experiences. These problems are not meant to be used as tools for blaming yourself or others for your suffering; they're supposed to offer you a learning experience for your inner growth.

Calmly Accept the Problem that Has Come into Your Life

At work, we tend to think analytically when we're trying to solve a problem. We analyze the problem from different angles by investigating the cause, separating the right from the wrong, and grouping our findings to help us find a way to solve the problem. This and various approaches to problem solving are the standard in corporate jobs and definitely essential skills that we want to have at work. But to look at life's problems from another, religious perspective, we ought to ask ourselves, "What is the meaning behind this problem? Why has this problem appeared in my life at this time?"

Please don't feel rushed into finding an answer. Your problem has emerged in your life for a reason, and you need to try to accept this.

When we fall ill, we need to make an effort to fight against the illness itself. We need to give ourselves a period of recuperation to heal our body and make other kinds of efforts too. But please do not deny that you've become ill. Instead, embrace your illness. Please accept into your heart that this issue has emerged at this point in the course of your life.

If you and your partner get into a huge argument, please accept this into your life. If you and your child are going through a rough patch in your relationship, please accept this, too. When you and your parents have a disagreement, just accept this. These problems may not necessarily be unique to you, and everyone is given their own problems in life to face. When a problem arises in your life, please calmly accept it as one among others in your workbook of life—the one that is being given to you to face right now.

3

There Are No Coincidences in This World

Let Your Mind Be Still and Cease Making Judgments about Your Problem

Please know that there are no coincidences in this world. Not all problems in life can be solved the same way we handle problems at work. The truth is that the path will open to you when you allow yourself to accept your problems. You may wonder why such a misery has befallen you after all the studying you've done, the love you've poured upon your family, the care you've devoted to your parents, or your many attractive qualities.

But what you must do is accept these circumstances calmly and then spend some time in meditation.

Cease your efforts to judge your problem; instead, just allow your mind to be still.

A mind that is anxious to reach a conclusion and constantly trying to judge the right as opposed to the wrong, the positive as opposed to the negative, progression as opposed to regression, a left turn as opposed to a right turn, and so on only creates additional suffering. When you find yourself in this state of mind, your first step should be to simply embrace everything that is happening to you. Refrain from trying to make judgments, and simply believe that it is the will of the universe that is presently unfolding. The meaning within it will come to light when it passes. That time may arrive while you are still in this world, or perhaps it will come after your departure from this world. You won't know exactly when it will come, but in the meantime, being able to accept everything that comes into your life, no matter what it may be, is an important life lesson to learn.

Feel the Will of the Great Universe in Your Meditation

Times of illness can teach us many important things.

They may warn us of imbalances in our mind and body, the inordinate expectations we have placed on ourselves, or the need to be more considerate of our relationships at home. Illness may also be a chance to realize the feelings that our ill mothers or fathers, whom we may previously have resented, went through during their times of sickness. Illness can also give us the time to understand the feelings of others or gain new perspectives on our work. As you can see, times of illness are sometimes necessary for our inner growth. Illness itself is not always an evil.

So when going through problems in life, let go of any thoughts for now that tell you that they are the results of a mistake. Stop blaming yourself or others, and embrace these problems. It's important to accept them as necessary experiences in your life and look upon them calmly in meditation. Let go of any judgment that arises in your mind. Don't be in a hurry to judge. This is not the time to make decisions about whether something is right or wrong, whether it's a sign to move forward or give up, or whether it should be kept or let go of.

Please calmly accept that what is arising in your life right now is necessary for you. The will of the great universe is at work, providing you with the problem that you need to face in your life right now, so what you must do is quietly embrace the purpose within it. Within it, you will surely find the necessary lessons for your spiritual training in this world. Your problems cannot be solved by your wish to protect yourself or with the problem-solving skills you use at work. Instead, you need to feel the will of the great universe, or the mind of God, in your heart.

We all wish that our lives could be smooth sailing, successful, and unburdened by problems. But no one among us in this world was born with a plan to live life flawlessly. Many pitfalls have been scattered throughout the course of our lives, but we cannot know about them in advance. If we were to know where these pitfalls lie, we would easily avoid them, and this would defeat their very purpose, which is to teach us important life lessons. Although this may seem like an unkindness, life's pitfalls are sprinkled upon our paths for us to stumble into.

When you find that you have tumbled into one, please don't think that this has happened by coincidence. This pitfall was prepared for you from the beginning, because this experience is necessary for you.

When you fall into a pitfall and land hard on your bottom, raise your gaze to the evening skies and ponder. Times like these are essential to our lives. We won't be able to discover who we truly are or understand other people's feelings in the truest sense without such experiences. Without these experiences, we might think that we see the world, when in truth we hardly do.

Some truths can only be understood over a lonely night of gazing at a starry sky. The great many people who supported us, the many times that we took their support for granted, and the numerous times we've taken credit that belonged to others—these are things that can only be realized when we're all alone with no one else to aid us. And when such feelings of fullness envelop us, we become one with the power of the great universe.

To Find Salvation, Let Go of Your Wish to Protect Yourself

In another sense, these experiences teach us to let go. The terms "selfish desires" and "the desire for self-preservation" are other ways that I have referred to our inner desire to protect ourselves. Feelings of self-love are something we all have, but we need to let go of these feelings. In place of them, we need to grow our capacity to accept and embrace our misfortunes and unhappiness. We need to believe that misfortunes and unhappiness do not happen to torture us, but to enlighten us with the wisdom we find as we resolve them. We need to believe that all problems will be resolved in the end.

There are things we fear every day. But only 1 percent or so of these fears will actually happen. It is the remaining 99 percent of our fears that we spend our lives worrying about. And by worrying about these various fears, we attract them into our reality as if to confirm the unhappiness of our lives.

In this way, we virtually become prophets of our own misery, predicting various kinds of misfortunes in our lives. We make predictions about our miserable future, dire financial circumstances, crumbling relationships, or looming divorce, as if to make such things come true. This is one wrong way that we use the power of our mind.

When you find yourself doing this, stop making judgments about your misfortune, and calmly accept it for the time being. To open yourself to salvation, you must try to find the will of the universe and let it lead you to your learning experience. When you are able to accept that your misfortunes arise because they're necessary to your life, you've already started on the road to salvation. When you surrender or relinquish the wish to protect yourself and determine to live as one with the will of the great universe, the path to salvation will surely open to you.

Stop Struggling and Simply Embrace Your Workbook of Life

This is similar to the technique we use to save ourselves from drowning. Flailing around too much may cause you to inhale water, which leads to drowning. But by not floundering and lying still, you allow your body to float naturally to the surface, and this works whether you're in a swimming pool or at the beach. Just stay still, allow your head to rise naturally to the water's surface, and allow the rest of your body to follow suit. The human body has less relative density than water, which is why we can be certain that we will float to the surface. It's when we flail our arms and end up inhaling water that many people drown.

So when you find yourself facing misfortune, please stop floundering and quietly accept the situation.

Seek to become one with the will of the great universe. When you do, salvation will come to you.

Become one with the universe and gracefully accept your workbook of life as it appears in front of you. Instead of blaming the problems you face on other people, your circumstances, your family, your job, or the government, simply accept that this problem is appearing now because it is necessary for you. When you do, you will already have begun to be at one with the will of the universe, and you will find your salvation about to manifest.

4

The Moment When We Feel the Miracle

Trust in the Lord's Will

To conclude, let us review everything I've talked about thus far. First, I said that we need to let go of everything. This means to put our trust in God, El Cantare. It is important for us to think in our hearts, "My Lord, my suffering is by no means the fault of others or a mistake on my part. Neither is it an act of God's unkindness. My suffering is here to teach me the meaning of the life that I was given in this world. I would like to accept this suffering and allow it to give me wisdom. This is why I wish to give this suffering over to you, my Lord."

You must stop struggling and trying to make a decision, and just accept your suffering instead. When you accept your suffering, you will feel yourself being uplifted. You will feel the power of your will to live burst forth from within you. And when you do, miracles will come to you.

Until then, it may feel like you've been suffering greatly despite your utmost individual efforts, and the world around you may seem like hell. You'll feel like you're struggling in a pit of despair, but you'll come to realize that this was not the case. Perhaps you thought that you had dived head first into the eddying tides of a whirlpool and were drowning, but then you realize that you were really just rolling around in your bed. Please put your trust in your higher power. When you do, your salvation will come to you without even realizing it.

Suffering Is a Gift of Compassion for Our Soul-Growth

In recent years, I've talked a lot about the importance of having faith. A truly developed faith should lead to the willingness to entrust everything to a higher power. This whole world exists under the will of the great universe, and nothing can truly be accomplished by our personal power alone.

The chance to be born into this world and to live our lives while experiencing soul training in this world is, in itself, something to be grateful for. In the true sense, there is nothing more we should ever want to ask for.

Please say these words in your heart: "Dear Lord, I want to hand over everything to you. If you believe that I need this experience for my soul training, then I will endure it. If this is necessary for my soul, then I will embrace it. I do not protest it. I do not resist it. I accept it as it is." When you find these feelings in your heart, you will realize that you have not been living in the pit of hell, but instead were being trained by life's greatest coach that exists.

Until we realize this, life feels as though we're in the midst of a painful hell. But in many cases in life, when we think that we are surrounded by heaven, we are actually surrounded by hell, and when we think we are surrounded by hell, we are actually in heaven. The truth is often the opposite of what we think it is.

You may now be feeling like you're suffering in the crucible of hell, but this is often the work of a great compassion that is encouraging your soul to grow stronger and to alchemize into pure gold. If you can come to believe in this truth, then just as the title of this chapter suggests, the moment when you will feel a miracle will certainly come to you.

Miracles Will Happen When You Become One with the Great Universe

Miracles won't happen when we try to use our personal power or ego to protect ourselves. Miracles don't occur when we strive to solve our problems using our human knowledge, experience, discernment, and effort to distinguish right from wrong.

Instead, miracles occur when we become one with the will of the great universe and give ourselves over to God. Please try to feel this miracle. Please make time for meditation, even if it's only fifteen minutes a day, for the chance to gain this experience. Please stop trying to solve problems at your own discretion. Instead accept them as they are. Accept what has appeared in front of you, and let yourself feel the miracle that is coming to you. When you do, you will see your state of mind beginning to change.

There are miracles happening in various places, including at Happy Science*, but there aren't that many yet, because we are trying to use our intellect, will, or emotions to solve our problems. But as we become one with the power of the great universe and give ourselves up to this power, many issues will be resolved. I sincerely hope that many people will be able to savor such moments of miracles in their lives.

Translator's Footnote

*Currently, through the power of faith, many people are experiencing miracles.

afterword

How interesting life is, that although I could perhaps have the most stressful life of any in this world, I am teaching others about becoming stress-free. In the thirty years since the day of my religious awakening, my life could have battered me with scars, but shifting my perspective toward giving love to others has made my body and soul as strong as diamonds.

To resolve our worries, we need to begin by dealing one by one with the various small problems that lie in front of us. By doing so, we create room to put our freedom and creativity to use. After that, what remains for us to do is wholeheartedly embrace the broader meaning of the destiny that heaven is sending us.

When you do this, you'll have the interesting experience of seeing that training your ability to work quickly ironically leads to protecting the spirituality of your mind. What you need to do is think of everything you do as for the sake of God.

Ryuho Okawa
Founder and CEO
Happy Science Group

The contents of this book were compiled from the following lectures given by Ryuho Okawa at a variety of Happy Science temples and locations.

Chapter 1
'Coping with Stress'
January 31, 2010
Matsudo Local Temple in Chiba Prefecture, Japan
(Japanese Title: 'Stress Management No Kotsu')

Chapter 2
'Improving Your Relationships'
August 12, 2011
Kitashinano Local Temple in Nagano Prefecture, Japan
(Japanese Title: 'Ningen Kankei Kojoho')

Chapter 3
'A Heart of Blessing'
April 12, 2005
General Headquarters in Tokyo, Japan
(Japanese Title: 'Shukufuku No Kokoro')

Chapter 4
'Living through the Giant Waves of Adversity'
June 1, 2008
Nagoya Chuo Local Temple in Aichi Prefecture, Japan, in the Nagoya Commemoration Hall (Japanese Title: 'Unmei No Onami Ni Momare Nagara Ikiru')

Chapter 5
'Feel the Miracle'
September 19, 2007
Oita Local Temple in Oita Prefecture, Japan
(Japanese Title: 'Kiseki Wo Kanjiyo')

about the author

Founder and CEO of Happy Science Group, Ryuho Okawa was born on 7 July 1956, in Tokushima, Japan. After graduating from the University of Tokyo with a law degree, he joined a Tokyo-based trading house. While working at its New York headquarters, he studied international finance at the Graduate Center of the City University of New York. In 1981, he attained Great Enlightenment and became aware that he is El Cantare with a mission to bring salvation to all humankind. In 1986, he established Happy Science. It now has members in 175 countries across the world, with more than 700 branches and temples as well as 10,000 missionary houses around the world.

He has given over 3,500 lectures (of which more than 150 are in English) and published over 3,200 books (of which more than 600 are Spiritual Interview Series), and many of which are translated into 42 languages. Along with The Laws of the Sun and The Laws of Hell, many of the books have become best sellers or million sellers. To date, Happy Science has produced 28 movies under the supervision of Okawa. He has given the original story and concept and is also the Executive Producer. He has also composed music and written lyrics of over 450 pieces.

Moreover, he is the Founder of Happy Science University and Happy Science Academy (Junior and Senior High School), Founder and President of the Happiness Realization Party, Founder and Honorary Headmaster of Happy Science Institute of Government and Management, Founder of IRH Press Co., Ltd., and the Chairperson of NEW STAR PRODUCTION Co., Ltd. and ARI Production Co., Ltd.

who is El Cantare?

El Cantare means "the Light of the Earth." He is the Supreme God of the Earth who has been guiding humankind since the beginning of Genesis, and He is the Creator of the universe. He is whom Jesus called Father and Muhammad called Allah, and is *Ame-no-Mioya-Gami*, Japanese Father God. Different parts of El Cantare's core consciousness have descended to Earth in the past, once as Alpha and another as Elohim. His branch spirits, such as Shakyamuni Buddha and Hermes, have descended to Earth many times and helped to flourish many civilizations. To unite various religions and to integrate various fields of study in order to build a new civilization on Earth, a part of the core consciousness has descended to Earth as Master Ryuho Okawa.

Alpha is a part of the core consciousness of El Cantare who descended to Earth around 330 million years ago. Alpha preached Earth's Truths to harmonize and unify Earth-born humans and space people who came from other planets.

Elohim is a part of the core consciousness of El Cantare who descended to Earth around 150 million years ago. He gave wisdom, mainly on the differences of light and darkness, good and evil.

Ame-no-Mioya-Gami (Japanese Father God) is the Creator God and the Father God who appears in the ancient literature, *Hotsuma Tsutae*. It is believed that He descended on the foothills of Mt. Fuji about 30,000 years ago and built the Fuji dynasty, which is the root of the Japanese civilization. With justice as the central pillar, Ame-no-Mioya-Gami's teachings spread to ancient civilizations of other countries in the world.

Shakyamuni Buddha was born as a prince into the Shakya Clan in India around 2,600 years ago. When he was 29 years old, he renounced the world and sought enlightenment. He later attained Great Enlightenment and founded Buddhism.

Hermes is one of the 12 Olympian gods in Greek mythology, but the spiritual Truth is that he taught the teachings of love and progress around 4,300 years ago which became the origin of the current Western civilization. He is a hero who truly existed.

Ophealis was born in Greece around 6,500 years ago and was the leader who took an expedition to as far as Egypt. He is the God of miracles, prosperity, and arts, and is known as Osiris in the Egyptian mythology.

Rient Arl Croud was born as a king of the ancient Incan Empire around 7,000 years ago and taught about the mysteries of the mind. In the heavenly world, he is responsible for the interactions that take place between various planets.

Thoth was an almighty leader who built the golden age of the Atlantic civilization around 12,000 years ago. In the Egyptian mythology, he is known as God Thoth.

Ra Mu was a leader who built the golden age of the civilization of Mu around 17,000 years ago. As a religious leader and a politician, he ruled by uniting religion and politics.

about Happy Science

Happy Science is a religious group founded on the faith in El Cantare who is the God of the Earth, and the Creator of the universe. The essence of human beings is the soul that was created by God, and we all are children of God. God is our true parent, so in our souls we have a fundamental desire to "believe in God, love God, and get closer to God." And, we can get closer to God by living with God's Will as our own. In Happy Science, we call this the "Exploration of Right Mind." More specifically, it means to practice the Fourfold Path, which consists of "Love,Wisdom, Self-Reflection and Progress."

Love: Love means "love that gives," or mercy. God hopes for the happiness of all people. Therefore, living with God's Will as our own means to start by practicing "love that gives."

Wisdom: By studying and putting spiritual knowledge into practice, you can cultivate wisdom and become better at resolving problems in life.

Self-Reflection: Once you learn the heart of God and the difference between His mind and yours, you should strive to bring your own mind closer to the mind of God—that process is called self-reflection. Self-reflection also includes meditation and prayer.

Progress: Since God hopes for the happiness of all people, you should also make progress in your love, and make an effort to realize utopia in which everyone in your society, country, and eventually all humankind can become happy.

As we practice this Fourfold Path, our souls will advance toward God step by step. That is when we can attain real happiness—our souls' desire to get closer to God comes true.

In Happy Science, we conduct activities to make ourselves happy through belief in Lord El Cantare, and to spread this faith to the world and bring happiness to all. We welcome you to join our activities!

We hold events and activities to help you practice the Fourfold Path at our branches, temples, missionary centers and missionary houses

Love: We hold various volunteering activities. Our members conduct missionary work together as the greatest practice of love.

Wisdom: We offer our comprehensive books collection, many of which are available online and at Happy Science locations. In addition, we give out numerous opportunities such as seminars or book clubs to learn the Truth.

Self-Reflection: We offer opportunities to polish your mind through self-reflection, meditation, and prayer. There are many cases in which members have experienced improvement in their human relationships by changing their own minds.

Progress: We also offer seminars to enhance your power of influence. Because it is also important to do well at work to make society better, we hold seminars to improve your work and management skills.

contact information

Happy Science is a worldwide organization with faith centers around the globe. For a comprehensive list of centers, visit the Worldwide Directory at
happy-science.org
okawabooks.com
The following are a few of the many Happy Science locations:

INTERNATIONAL HQ
Tokyo
1-6-7 Togoshi,Shinagawa,
Tokyo 142-0041, Japan
Tel: 81-3-6384-5770
Fax: 81-3-6384-5776
Email: tokyo@happy-science.org
Website: www.happy-science.org

INDIA
Delhi
Email: newdelhi@happy-science.org
Tel: 91-98738-36008

Mumbai
Email: mumbai@happy-science.org
Tel: 91-98192-64400

Aurangabad
Email: aurangabad@happy-science.org
Tel: 91-89561-01911

Tamil Nadu
Email: tamilnadu@happy-science.org
Tel: 91-98192-64400
Chennai: 91-98215-49437

Kolkata
Email: kolkata@happy-science.org
Tel: 91-82928-24767

Bodh Gaya
Email: bodhgaya@happy-science.org
Tel: 91-82928-24767

SRI LANKA
Colombo
Ground Floor No. 255,
Dr. N.M. Parera Mawatha,
Colombo 08
Email: srilanka@happy-science.org
Tel: 94-71-1544536

NEPAL
Kathmandu Metropolitan City,
Ward No.15, Ring Road, Kimdol,
Sitapaila Kathmandu, Nepal
Email: nepal@happy-science.org
Tel: 977-1-5372931